A Dad's *Fun Guide* to

Raising Happy Daughters

A Dad's _Fun Guide_ to Raising Happy Daughters

Imagination Activities Against Body-Snatching Zombie Naysayers and Other Foes of Happiness

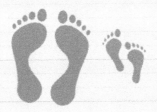

JOHN GRIFFITH

Edited by Ralph Zuranski

Artistic Design by Mark Foster

Cover by Jason Vaughn

Publisher

John Griffith, LLC

A Dad's <u>Fun Guide</u> to Raising Happy Daughters; *Imagination Activities Against Body-Snatching Zombie Naysayers and Other Foes of Happiness*

ISBN: 978-0-692-89931-1
First Edition

Published by John Griffith, LLC, McKinney, TX.

Index written by Sue Klefstad.

eBook formatting by Booknook.biz.

Cover photo courtesy of bluelela/shutterstock.com.

Some images provided by Shutterstock.com.
Used by Permission.

Some images provided by Pixabay.com.
Used by Permission.

Scripture from THE HOLY BIBLE, NEW INTERNATIONAL VERSION ®,
NIV ® Copyright © 1973, 1978, 1984, 2011 by Biblica, Inc. ®
Used by permission. All rights reserved worldwide.

First 9 lines of Chapter 2 from TAO TE CHING BY LAO TZU, A NEW ENGLISH VERSION, WITH FOREWORD AND NOTES, by STEPHEN MITHCELL. Translation copyright © 1988 by Stephen Mitchell. Reprinted by permission of HarperCollins Publishers.

Hot Potato
Words & Music by Murray Cook, Jeff Fatt, Anthony Field, John Field, Greg Page
© 1994 Wiggly Tunes Pty Ltd
Used by Permission.

For my Princesses

Dedication

I wrote this book for myself and my three daughters. It started out as a book of healing our way out of a "big old pile of crap," but it evolved. "Big pile of crap," ... gone. This book is now the stuff of magic. It is for dads of daughters.

When fathers are actively involved in the lives of their daughters, magic happens. Both dads and their daughters benefit. Good magic! Indescribable magic.

Girls! For the last 18 years, I have been raising those sweet-smelling princesses. They glisten instead of sweat. They always brush their teeth twice a day. They don't fart. "Righhhht."

They stink when they sweat. At least one of my girls does not like brushing her teeth. And collectively speaking, they fart nearly continuously. My youngest is five. My oldest is eighteen. I have one more sandwiched in between.

My girls are not "perfect." I am not "perfect."

Guess what? It is not about "being perfect." It's about love. Nobody is "perfect." But, everyone is in the "perfect place" in their life at any given moment.

With me raising them, I continue to learn from my girls. They are still revealing to me what I need to know, so that I can teach them.

As long as there is air in our lungs, we will actively participate in each other's lives. Sure, as they grow older, the need for "fathering" decreases. But, I will always be their dad, and they will always be my daughters.

The words "their dad" does not imply that they are treated as a group. Each daughter demands that I am her very own, personalized, one-of-a-kind dad. And of course, each daughter goes out of her way to demand that personalized approach.

"Dad, I am nothing like my sisters. Pay special attention to me!"

There will never be a milestone date when we cut our ties from one another and close the door.

I don't get that. Besides, I have to make sure that they are going to return a very special favor someday, changing my diapers when I am old. I will depend on them for many needs at the end of my days, just like they depended on me "pampering" them at the beginning of theirs.

Who else should read this book? Oprah! Yes, I have said on more than one occasion to my middle daughter, "Oprah is going to read this, and she is going to love it, and I am going to meet her to talk about it. When I do, I will take you and your sisters with me to meet her."

Meeting Oprah means millions of people are going to read this, and I believe that would be a very good thing.

"Oh, my goodness, that would be a good thing in 'O' so many ways."

Oprah, I am just throwing this idea of us meeting one day out there. I am planting seeds. I teach my daughters, "Ask! Ask for anything you desire." By the way, I love how your last name says "win" and "free."

This book is dedicated to dads, moms, and you, Oprah.

Foreword by Ralph Zuranski

John Griffith is a paragon of fatherhood. He is a model of excellence, when it comes to raising three daughters as a single dad. His book, "A Dad's <u>Fun Guide</u> to Raising Happy Daughters; *Imagination Activities Against Body-Snatching Zombie Naysayers and Other Foes of Happiness*" is amazing. It helped me better understand the love, sacrifice, and wisdom necessary to raise children in this new millennium.

This book is not just for dads; but also, moms, aunts and uncles raising nieces and nephews, grandparents raising grandkids, teachers, counselors, probation officers, and people of faith. If you are raising or mentoring one or more children, this book provides you with valuable advice, tips, tools, exercises and most importantly, encouragement.

Hi, my name is Ralph Zuranski, a former reporter for the "Coronado Eagle Journal," in San Diego. It is a local newspaper on Coronado Island, a small city across the bay from downtown San Diego. It is the home of the Naval Amphibious Base, the home of the SEALS, and North Island Naval Air Station.

I have a deep admiration and respect for all the members of the military and their families. I have a soft spot in my heart for military families and the challenges they face because my parents, uncles, and aunts all served our country in World War II.

My dad even survived the crash of a B26 bomber after a bombing mission in Germany. My uncle Jerry received two Bronze stars in the Battle of the Bulge.

As a reporter, I had the opportunity to meet and interview many of our military heroes and their families. Few realize the major sacrifices required by these fathers and mothers who raise their children under very difficult circumstances.

In 1992, community leaders in the Rotary Club and Chamber of Commerce, reporters at Coronado Cablevision and KNSD TV stations and the principal and teachers at Coronado high school, helped me create and coordinate the "In Search of Heroes" research program. The goal was to inspire local high school journalism students to go in search of heroes, to discover who really are the unsung heroes in our society.

The results were astonishing. Eighty percent of the time, moms were identified as the heroes who do not get the recognition and rewards they so richly deserve. They sacrifice their time, talent, physical health, emotional well-being, and treasure to raise their children, especially when the dads are not around.

Twenty-five years later, the world has definitely changed. Men, whether married or single, are taking on a more proactive role as the primary parent.

This is good news! Historically, women were expected to raise children. They were trapped in the Caregiver role. Moms were the pillows and the bandages.

Men were the workplace and military warriors who insured their wives and children had food, clothing, shelter, and education. Dads hammered out a living for their family in the cruel, hard, dog-eat-dog business world.

Over the last 10 years, there has been a movement towards gender equality. One or both parents may be deployed for many weeks, to military hotspots around the globe. Men are now choosing to raise their children, when the moms are deployed or absent from the home.

After editing John's book, I realized he is a unique "single-parent Hero." His insights helped me gain an appreciation, admiration, and respect for single and married fathers who raise their children. Their daily challenge to provide food, clothing, shelter, education, entertainment, guidance, inspiration, and most importantly unconditional love, is astounding.

John has inspired me to reactivate the "In Search of Heroes" research program. I want to find out, if the "hero-gap" between dads and moms has changed.

Now, we are encouraging high school journalism students to video the interviews of their heroes, and post them to the "In Search of Heroes" YouTube Channel: https://www.youtube.com/c/insearchofheroes. Then we can all vote for the most inspirational heroes and best interviews by journalism students.

John Griffith's book is dedicated to all families dealing with the difficult circumstances of raising children. In this hectic, hostile and fast-paced world, every head of a family, with one or two parents, will find the principles in the book useful.

The book provides you with valuable insights, concrete advice and entertaining lessons that help you deal with and triumph over the challenges of parenthood. Read the book with your children so together you can learn about and apply the profound insights to your unique family situation.

I must admit that I am a better grandfather to three granddaughters because of what I learned from John Griffith. I highly recommend his book, "A Dad's Fun Guide to Raising Happy Daughters; *Imagination Activities Against Body-Snatching Zombie Naysayers and Other Foes of Happiness.*" It is a valuable resource in my grandparenting library.

Contents

Preface

A BIT ABOUT MY "DAD-STYLE"

This is my first book. It is an expression of love and fatherly guidance to my three daughters. I pray you find this information entertaining, informative, and valuable in your daughter raising journey.

When I think about it, my entire life as their father is an expression of love and guidance manifesting through the experiences my daughters and I share. It does not matter *what* we experience together. It only matters *that* we experience together.

As a dad, I have my own one-of-a-kind style that is very consistent. I am connector of dots, that may not even be intentionally present. I look for hidden meanings and messages that may be useful in life. I encourage my daughters to ask "Why?" But more than anything else, I make life fun. This is true when I am working on sight words with my little one, watching a movie with my middle one, or coaching automobile driving skills with my oldest. Every moment we share is an opportunity for insight and fun.

As you can imagine, this dad-style of mine requires a healthy flow of words from my mouth. My daughters would say I talk a lot. But don't be fooled, they love the fact that I yack.

I also "listen." I listen to their words, their moods, their energy, and their expressions. My daughters would say that I think and analyze a lot. They love this about me too, except on those days when they want to be inward and private. On those days, they probably wish I had the intuition of a rock.

This book is written true to form of my style as a dad. Amidst me sharing the history of the modern zombie, explaining the processes of the water cycle or making the case that Benjamin Franklin was one cool dude, there is frequent interjecting of commentary, insight, dot-connecting, questioning and humor.

It is almost as if there are two voices in this book – me as the author and me as Dad – bouncing back and forth. In order to make this book easier to read as well as avoid any perceptions that I might have a split personality, I chose to use *italics* for my Dad voice.

WARNING, THIS BOOK IS RATED PG

Don't say I did not warn you. This book is intentionally "edgy." By that, I mean that it is a bit offbeat, unique, and gritty. At times, you might find my style offensive or refreshing, or both. If you are okay being challenged with opening your mind to new perspectives, then forge ahead.

There aren't any cuss words in this book, but it does contain a few of those "^#$%&" funny symbols where cuss words would otherwise be spoken. There are also occasional mentions of body excretions like spit, pee, and poop. There are also some references to body parts such as boobs and brains.

There are fun discussions about "controversial" topics such as miracles, time travel, socialism, body snatching and more. There is also some science, Yikes!

Oh, I almost forgot. I must warn you about one last thing. "This book also refers to God, quite a bit."

Introduction

THE PIECES AND PARTS OF THIS BOOK

I f you are reading this, you are reading the introduction. That is amazing. I usually skip introductions. I won't anymore, because now I know they are important. Kudos to you.

The next section, Part 1, "The Day I Became a King," is about my life from childhood through the day my first daughter was born. By definition, a princess is the daughter of a monarch or king. And from the moment she was born, that little girl was definitely a princess. That made me by default, a king.

Scary!

By king, I don't mean some arrogant, "bow-down-and-kiss-my-ring" or "kiss-my ..." followed by a "word-that-rhymes-with-gas" type king. I also don't mean the type of king that beheads others that don't agree with him. *That is a bit extreme.*

Nor, do I mean a king that taxes the poor to fuel a life of lust and excess.

No, I am not talking about those types of kings. I am talking about a good king. I am talking about a king who:
• leads by example.
• exhibits good character.
• teaches, uplifts and protects others.
• helps others reach their full potential.
• finds gratitude in any situation.
• makes himself available to those in need, even if it means barely sleeping.
• seeks to understand.
• provides for others.
• is ultra-intuitive.
• discerns the minds of others when words fail them.
• is loyal and supportive.
• fosters the well-being and personal growth of others.
• makes loving decisions.
• believes that happiness is a birthright for all.
• enjoys having fun, and is playful.

This good type of king is a lot like "Well, Hmmm, Gosh!" a good dad. King or Dad, I was a most unlikely candidate for either.

Scary, I tell you, scary.

Part 2, "My Darling Daughter, You Awakened Me!" is about how I ultimately came to realize that the life I was experiencing was not the life I was meant to live. This revelation was triggered by my first daughter's birth and the next few weeks of her "wee, wittle life," when she cracked her first smile.

On that day, when she smiled for the first time, she levelled me. She knocked me flat on my back with a jab, followed by a heavy cross, then a hook, and finally finishing me off with an uppercut. She was Muhammad Ali. I was me.

When I came back to consciousness after that knock-out combo, I knew then that the life I was experiencing was upside down. I thought to myself, "Why would any living creature want to live if the longer they live, the worse it gets?"

Seriously. Think about that for a moment. Plants don't bloom on day one. They must grow first before they produce glorious flowers.

Ok, great! I knew my life was way off course. But, I had no idea how it happened, why, or how to fix it. But that was okay. A seeking heart always finds an answer. My heart was not just seeking, it was hunting. Over the next 15 years and with eventually three daughters, the answers came to me one by one.

Part 3, "Seven Keys to Happiness" is a seven-chapter collection of those very answers, expressed in my own unique style of "dad speak" to my daughters. Each chapter has two sections.

The first section of each chapter is an educational explanation covering a variety of topics including history, religion, science, art, philosophy, spirituality, literature and pop-culture.

These educational "stories" are expressed with humor obviously. I lose my daughters' attention the minute they hear the word "history." Immediately their thoughts go to old, fat bald guys that wear wigs. Shortly thereafter, their eyelids begin to close, and saliva begins to collect in their mouths for the drool that is soon to fall.

Hidden within each story is one of the "Seven Keys to Happiness" revelations I experienced while raising my daughters.

The second section of each chapter is a love letter from me, revealing the previous section's hidden secret in my "one-of-a-kind" dad style."

Part 4, "Fun Things to do Together" contains an activity for each of the seven keys from Part 3. The activities include art, journaling, science experiments and more. They are loads of fun to do with your daughter or daughters.

These activities help you and your daughter understand and apply each "Key to Happiness," but in a completely different way.

My daughters need some balance in how they receive information from me. Did I tell you that they think I talk too much sometimes? Oh, and they also think I repeat myself.

WHY THIS BOOK?

I love my daughters infinitely. Tomorrow, I will love them even more. Without hesitation, I would give my life to save theirs. I live much of my life for them.

Why? Because it makes me happy. Happiness is the purpose of life. It's a gift. Sadly, most of us "sheeple" don't know how to receive that gift. I didn't.

"Sheeple" is a blending of the words "people" and "sheep," and describes the masses of people who tend to follow what everyone else is doing, or what they are being told to do (or believe) by powerful influencers.

Just like sheep, we tend to follow the flock. I see a lot of unhappiness in the flock, with a correlation between age and unhappiness. The younger someone is, the happier they generally are.

That's kind of screwed up.

Society, unintentionally, works against our happiness. We are constantly bombarded by a stream of "Bad News." We are encouraged to find power in suffering and entitlement, rather than in choice and taking personal responsibility for our own happiness.

Getting even, keeping score, making others pay and getting away with lying and cheating are common themes on network television shows. Escaping reality through addictive and destructive behaviors is glamorized, romanticized and sensationalized.

We sheeple swallow this information, and gradually drift away from the happiness we once knew.

Of course, you know, "We become what we consume and absorb both intellectually and physically," which is a fancy way of saying "We are what we eat."

My daughters righted my course. They helped me rediscover the gift of a happy life, a gift I too lost as I grew older. Now I am giving that same gift back to them in a way that I know they will understand, a "dad's way." Should my daughters veer off course as they grow older, I want them to know the way back. That, is why I wrote this book.

These are not your typical "daddy daughter" lessons, but they can be. Even though I occasionally see each one of my daughters latch on to some "stinking thinking" patterns, they always get out of it using these lessons.

This astounds me. It shouldn't, but it does. This works. It worked for me, it is working for them, and it can work for you and your daughter.

SHARING THOUGHTS

I have read all of Part 3 to my older girls. We also did the activities together in Part 4. I teach these same lessons to my little one, but in a manner more appropriate for her age. I encourage you to do the same with your daughter or daughters, in a style that works for you.

Regardless of the age of my daughters, the message is consistent. These are important life lessons and skills that are seldom discussed with our children.

Ultimately, all of these life skills can be boiled down into one concept. "You only have complete control of your thoughts and feelings, but that is ok. It just so happens that the most powerful force available to us, is our thoughts."

The power of thought is a spiritual law, that is as real and consistent as gravity.

Choose your thoughts, because your life will follow them. Crappy thoughts create a crappy life. Good thoughts, a good life. It is the only way life unfolds. There is no exception. It is law.

The most important thing we dads can do is to be actively engaged in our daughter's life, and teach these life skills. I do this, because it brings me great happiness. I do it as an expression of love.

Expressing love to my daughters enriches my life. Receiving love enriches the life of each of my daughters. And the chances are very good that they will do the same for their own children someday. How can that be anything but good?

You know, that is the way love works. The lover loves, because loving is joyful. The loved one receives the wonderful gift of being loved. The loved one becomes a lover and loves others. On and on love spreads, across the here-and-now and into the future lives of our children's children. Powerful stuff.

Dads, you matter more to your daughter than you can really imagine. You have the opportunity to be the single most important male role model in your daughter's life. Thank you for letting me share this book with you. I hope you have as much fun reading this book as I had writing it.

PART 1

The Day I Became a King

ME BEFORE HER

I grew up in a family of four boys, experiencing broken limbs, stitches, bloody noses, busted lips and broken teeth. I crashed my bicycle many times trying to reproduce the stunts of Evel Knievel. I can tell you from personal experience, that it hurts deep inside when you fall off the roof of a house.

I had at least one fight with every kid in the neighborhood close to my age. I accidentally broke windows with baseballs, wiffle-balls and basketballs. I started a few fires that got out of control. I can count at least 4 times I escaped serious danger or death.

Looking back, I sometimes wonder if all boys have these types of dangerous stories. Let me tell you about mine.

My first escape was from drowning. A close friend and I were in a rowboat in the middle of Lake Brownwood in west Texas. We were not wearing life jackets.

That was dumb.

It was a clear day, until a thunderstorm rolled in without warning.

That is Texas weather for you.

The waves began rising and falling, tossing our boat around like a toy in a raging maelstrom. The thunder boomed and lightning struck.

A very scary situation.

We were soaked to the bone, the boat awash with rain and pee.

To make matters worse, my friend fell on the bottom of the rowboat in a fetal position and began to cry. He screamed repeatedly, "We are going to die! We are going to die!" With every ounce of strength I could muster, I single-handedly rowed us back to shore. Our friendship was never the same after that frightening experience.

Speaking of jackets, let me tell you my escape from a swarm of yellow jacket wasps. It goes without saying, but I will say it anyway. "Yellow jacket nests make terrible dinner bells."

Our family was at a small lake in the country for a picnic. My mom, or maybe my aunt, asked me to call my brothers and cousins to eat.

Earlier that day, I had noticed hanging from an old oak tree, a large and cool looking old bell. Growing up in west Texas, I had learned all about chuck wagons, and the way those cooks rounded up the cowboys for a meal, by ringing a bell. I even had participated in several chuck wagon dinner field trips.

So, what was a boy to do? Heck yes, I was going to ring that bell. So I did, without first looking inside the bell. I grabbed the clapper and swung it back and forth with all my chuck wagon might.

I should have looked inside.

I wanted to yodel the words "dinner is served" but instead I screamed like a Banshee. You see, I was swarmed by some very pissed-off yellow jackets that lived inside the bell.

Of course, they were pissed! I just delivered an earthquake on the magnitude of eight to those yellow jackets.

I screamed like a baby as those yellow jackets plunged their stingers into my arm. Even though there were no words coming out of my mouth, my dad understood exactly what I was saying.

He raced over to me, threw me on his shoulder and ran for the lake. I am pretty sure he got stung too, but my dad was tough as nails.

My arm soon blew up like a basketball. I felt sick, sick, sick. That day was "no picnic" for me. I now look in unfamiliar spaces before I reach in with my hands. *My dad had always cautioned me about this. On that day, I understood why.*

Speaking of ringing bells, let me tell you about the time I barely escaped from getting my bell rung by the bumper of a car. I had developed this new form of running that made me fly like the wind. The technique was perfectly aerodynamic. Instead of clinching my fists into a ball, I held them out straight like karate hands.

We were at a ballpark watching one of my older brothers play baseball. When the game concluded, I decided to put on the karate-jets and dash to my mother's car about 50 yards away and across a street.

I engaged my karate hands and exploded like a rocket. I was fast, I might have even heard a sonic boom!

My eyes were fixed on the finish line, my mom's gold station wagon. I think I mentioned that her car was parked *across* the street, right?

When I came to the street, I did not stop. I did not even look both ways.

That was dumb.

I was in the zone, running my very best. Suddenly, my focus was rudely interrupted. The sound of screeching tires and my screaming mom caused me to assume the fetal position. I collapsed like a blob in the middle of the street, sobbing and squirming. The car stopped miraculously inches from my face.

The driver leaped out of the car to see if I was ok.

Poor guy, he was a basket case.

My mom scooped me up from the street and carried me to the finish line.

Poor mom, she was a basket case too.

I rode home with my head in my mom's lap, sobbing and shuddering the entire way. My older brother of course dug in to me with that "special loving kindness," that older brothers are so good at expressing!

Now I look both ways all the time. *My mom and dad had always cautioned me to look both ways. This day, I understood why.*

Speaking of guys driving cars and dangerous situations, let me tell you about my escape from a dangerous, creepy guy driving a car. In the summer of fourth grade, I frequently crossed paths with a guy driving an old, oversized car. He was the epitome of "stranger danger." There was nothing subtle in the way he tried to coax me over to his car.

Fortunately, I had training. My elementary school had hosted a school-wide presentation by law enforcement. They taught us what and what not to do with creeps like this guy.

Focused messaging on any topic has an impact on kids. When we take it seriously, they take it seriously.

Using my training, I had no problem evading him by racing off in the opposite direction from his car toward the largest crowd of people.

One day I was approaching the right hand turn on to 56th street where I lived. I noticed out of my periphery the creepy guy in his car, slowly rolling next to me. "Creepster" was traveling in the same direction!

I glanced to the left for a split second to assess the situation. Creepy guy was leaning across his front seat, staring at me out of the passenger window! I looked away and started walking faster. My street was just a short distance, so I decided to make a break for it rather than turn in the opposite direction, as I had been taught.

My muscles were ready for the karate-style run of my life. But, before I could fire my muscles, an empty bottle of booze slammed against a wall near my head.

The bottle shattered into a million razor-sharp shards of glass, covering the sidewalk. The smell of liquor filled the air. Creepy guy had tried to knock me out by hurling a bottle at me through his car window! I feared for my life. A massive dose of adrenaline flooded into my bloodstream, causing my muscles to explode into action. I took off running faster than ever before, faster than my ballpark dash.

In a flash, I turned right on to 56th street, safe at last as creepy guy punched the accelerator and sped away. I never saw him again.

I was just a normal boy, living a normal boy's life.

My poor mom and dad, they had four of us. Of course, in my mind I was the easiest.

I also did other normal boy things, like sports.

I hit home-runs, made impossible hook shots in basketball, and executed perfect twisting flips from the high diving board. I was an all-star in all the sports I played.

I was a big fan of "GI-Joe," so of course I loved waging war. Enemy number one was the glorious vocalist of west Texas, the cicada. I sniped those singing cicadas from the ground below with a BB Gun.

I am ashamed of the slaughter.

I routinely laid waste to red ant beds with smoke bombs, firecrackers, lighter fluid and matches.

Ditto on the shame.

I also was very good at imprisoning those head-poking ground squirrels in buckets, after flooding their homes with about 25 gallons of water. Sure, I pissed them off but I did not take their life.

Just a little shame.

I made high grades in school, and was considered a good student and citizen by all of the teachers. I went to church most Sundays at St. John's and was convinced the church was named after me. Also, I was obsessed with learning to play the piano at the age of ten, and I still play to this day.

My head was full of dreams during those years. I knew that I could do or be anything I wanted. I also knew that I was immortal.

If a prophet told me "You will spend most of your life surrounded by girls!" I would have said "Yuck. Girls are gross. Girls have girl germs."

And that is what my life was like through the sixth grade. I was just a normal boy. Then came grades seven through twelve.

Junior high and high school were very different. Something was going on inside of me. In junior high, my voice started crackling like a cross between a goose and a donkey.

My nipples became hard, enlarged and sore. They were perfect targets for my older brothers' thumping fingers.

New juices in my body made me "cra cra." *I learned that word from my daughters. It means crazy. See how cool I am?*

The world appeared in an entirely different light. And, those gross girls from elementary school were suddenly, not so gross.

For the next six years, navigating the social circles became priority "numero uno." I frequently checked myself for bad breath, boogers, body odor, pepper in my teeth, and pee drips on my pants on days I wore khakis.

I tried like crazy to keep any form of gas from sneaking out of my orifices. On the occasion a fart slipped out in the presence of a girl. Of course, I blamed the closest poor male soul standing near me.

If there was no one around but a girl, I pretended it never happened. But inside, of course, I died. If there was an odor, then "kill me now." My "coolness quotient" was my primary concern. I needed to look hot, smell good, act "fly." *I learned that word from my daughters too! It means 'cool.'*

I still loved waging war, but now the enemy was pimples, zits and blackheads. My former insect and animal foes were grateful for the ceasefire.

As before, I did well in school. I was student body officer, outstanding citizen, "blah blah blah." I sang in the choir, played sports, won awards, "blah blah blah."

My piano skills were vastly improved and despite my weirdly changing voice, I could sing. I also started writing music.

By the way, that pianist, vocalist, composer combo served me very well in my newfound pursuit of the girlies.

If a prophet told me "You will spend most of your life surrounded by girls!" I would have said, "Cool! I like girls!" I was just a normal boy.

And that is what my life was like through junior high and high school. Then came college.

In college, I searched for the meaning of life. I became deeply philosophical. I questioned everything including my own existence. I soaked up "knowledge" like a sponge. I grew my hair and beard long. I lived on cheap Thai food and coffee.

Some days I believed in God, others I did not. No matter what I believed on any given day, I was always right.

I graduated from college with Magna Cum Laude status. History, math, music, art, religion, science, and psychology were my focus. I thought I knew everything, but in reality, knew nothing.

If a prophet told me, "You will spend most of your life surrounded by girls!" I would have said, "I have no time for girls, at least not any particular girl, for I am a free spirit." I was just a normal college boy. The next 12 years is where things really got interesting.

After college, I did not start a career or settle down in a home with a wife and kids. I did not do anything that many people do after college. I did not obtain health insurance. Instead, I chose to find myself.

In my pursuit of myself, paying the bills eventually became difficult. I lived like a vagabond, eking out a meager daily living. I wrote data driven computer programs for pennies on the dollar, played piano at happy hours for even less money, and actually paid money to grind out rock and roll on the weekends, after settling my tab.

I grew leaps and bounds, never finding myself. I made many "so-called friends" I never see. Unfortunately, I also indulged in unmentionable things, creating a great deal of collateral damage in the lives of others.

If you happen to be one of those people I hurt during those years, I am sincerely sorry and ask your forgiveness.

As the years ticked by, the daily struggle and stress of living increased. All of my creativity, talent and knowledge was applied toward survival. I no longer had dreams or believed I could do or be anything. I no longer believed in my immortality. I could hardly see past tomorrow.

My life sucked and I knew it. Yet, I did not see a need to make a change. Instead, I accepted that, "This is just how life is!" I settled comfortably in to numbness. I had become what Pink Floyd expressed in their rock and roll classic "Comfortably Numb," from *The Wall*.

The last 8 lines of that song describe a child that had dreams. But when the child grew up, the dreams went away. Living life with enthusiasm was replaced with apathy and acceptance that life was not joyful. The grown child – now a man – no longer cared, that at one time he cared. He was numb, and comfortable with being numb.

If a prophet told me, "You will spend most of your life surrounded by girls!" I would have said, "That is not possible. I don't think there is much life left for me to live."

And then, my life changed.

THE RETURN OF THE PRODIGAL SON

I did meet a girl, surprisingly enough. As it turns out, she would play a very important role in the prophecy coming true. We found our way into one another's life in early 1997. In July 1997, we learned we were going to have a child. Despite this news, I continued living a lost life.

I was involved during the pregnancy from the very beginning. I attended doctor visits, sonograms, and served a very emotional and physically uncomfortable "mom-in-waiting" the best I could.

But my spirit and my mind were disengaged. I really didn't "feel" the gravity of the situation. Honestly, I knew a child was coming, but I did not believe it.

The sonogram revealed she was a girl. Maternity science projected her date of birth to be March 23, 1998. On March 1, 22 days before she was to be born, my life and perspective changed. Not a little, a lot. The gravity of the situation suddenly became overwhelming. I felt it in my heart and soul. She was coming! That day, March 1, unfolded in a most incredible manner.

Some event that I cannot recall exactly, caused me to read the parable of the prodigal son, from the book of Luke. I was very familiar with this parable. I had read it many times.

This time however, it seemed completely different. The words resonated. The message felt personal.

The parable was all about me. It affected me profoundly.

> [11] "Jesus continued: "There was a man who had two sons. [12] The younger one said to his father, 'Father, give me my share of the estate.' So, he divided his property between them.

> [13] "Not long after that, the younger son got together all he had, set off for a distant country and there squandered his wealth in wild living. [14] After he had spent everything, there was a severe famine in that whole country, and he began to be in need. [15] So he went and hired himself out to a citizen of that country, who sent him to his fields to feed pigs. [16] He longed to fill his stomach with the pods that the pigs were eating, but no one gave him anything.

> [17] "When he came to his senses, he said, 'How many of my father's hired servants have food to spare, and here I am starving to death! [18] I will set out and go back to my father and say to him: [19] Father, I have sinned against heaven and against you. I am no longer worthy to be called your son; make me like one of your hired servants.' [20] So he got up and went to his father.

"But while he was still a long way off, his father saw him and was filled with compassion for him; he ran to his son, threw his arms around him and kissed him." (New International Version, Luke 15.11-20).

STOP!!!

There is more to this parable, but it is the words in verse 20 that gave me hope. That wayward son was a long way off in a faraway land. He was willing to eat the food of pigs. He was at an all-time low and had finally hit the bottom. In his most miserable state ever, he turned around and decided to return home to his father.

That son was out of sight, yet his father "saw" him. That son had made no measurable progress on his return, but his father did not care. The son merely turned around and decided to return home, and that was enough for his father. And what did the father do?

His father did not stay put. He ran toward his son. He shortened the distance. He did not punish his son. He did not place conditions on his return. Let's look at the next few verses.

> [21] "The son said to him, 'Father, I have sinned against heaven and against you. I am no longer worthy to be called your son.'
> [22] "But the father said to his servants, 'Quick! Bring the best robe and put it on him. Put a ring on his finger and sandals on his feet. [23] Bring the fattened calf and kill it. Let's have a feast and celebrate. [24] For

this son of mine was dead and is alive again; he was lost and is found.' So they began to celebrate."
(New International Version, Luke 15.21-24).

His father celebrated, threw his arms around his son, kissed him, and threw a party.

I cried, and then cried some more. On March 1, I had finally come to the end of myself. I decided to turn my life around. I was going to be a father of a baby girl in just 22 days. I did not know what in the heck to do next. I only knew that I was going to change my life. And, thus, the countdown began.

THE COUNTDOWN

Have you ever noticed we count up in some cases, and down in others? When we play Hide and Go Seek, we count up. On New Year's Eve or when we launch rockets into space, we count down. The two counting directions feel very different.

Counting up, whether marking an end or beginning, lacks oomph. It feels less anxious, less monumental.

Sorry soccer fans. The end of your games has no pop. They just whimper to conclusion.

Counting down on the other hand feels cataclysmic. When the countdown reaches zero, something grand occurs. The event might be destructive, creative, or both, but it is always big.

When the New Year arrives and the countdown hits zero, we feel released from the previous year's difficulties. We look to the New Year with hope. The slate is clean and a new year is born. The previous year is officially done.

This is a big deal.

We countdown when we launch rockets also. The rocket fuel explodes in a blinding, thundering mass of fire, smoke, and destruction. And then, a rocket emerges, thrusting into space to send mankind into the unknown.

This is a big deal.

The countdown for the arrival of my first daughter started on March 1, 22 days before her birth. I was scared, drifting, aimless. Yet, even after the few hours since I decided to change the direction of my life, I knew I was heading in the right direction.

I could feel it.

And, just as the father raced toward his son in the parable, unconditional love raced toward me. Still, I had no idea what to do next. I was as they say, "Freaking out!" And then, I listened to my calm inner voice, "Ask. Just ask." So, I did just that.

I found a pen, a piece of paper and an envelope. With tears streaming down my cheeks, I wrote the following letter to a God who I mostly ignored for the last 12 years.

"Dear God. I have lived a selfish life. I have done nothing to prepare for the birth of my daughter. Please God, just let her be healthy. I promise I will be an amazing father. I will be the dad she deserves. I will be the best dad she could ever have. Please God, just give me this chance!"

I folded my tear soaked letter and sealed it in the envelope. Within seconds, I heard another voice. This voice was not calm at all. This voice was full of panic. The voice did not come from within, as before. This voice was coming from the next room!

The mother-to-be of my daughter screamed, "My water broke!" My baby was on her way. The countdown from 22 to zero days was now compressed in to hours.

On March 2, my first daughter was born. She was three weeks early and weighed just a little over five pounds. She was perfect. And, this was a big deal, bigger than rockets or New Year's Day. A princess was born. That made me a king, one of those good kings, her Dad.

The prophet was right. I was indeed going to spend my life surrounded by girls, three daughters eventually. What an amazing and wonderful life it has been.

FAST FORWARD TO TODAY

Today, I am blessed with three amazing daughters, separated by no less than five years between each. None of my daughters will ever share the same phase of "girlhood" at the same time.

Just like daughter one, daughters two and three wasted no time teaching me how to be "her" dad! However, that is where the similarities stopped.

The lessons of each daughter were very different. They all were and still are very unique in their approach in teaching me how to be "her" dad. Each one demands my exclusive attention, and I joyfully comply.

For most of their lives, I have been a single dad. I am their primary provider and caregiver. While it might be less common for a father to be the "primary parent" for little girls, it certainly is not a disadvantage or a handicap.

My middle daughter asked me the other day, "What do little newborn babies dream about?" I thought about it for a moment. Then, I held my hands up and made a circle about six inches across.

I answered jokingly, "Honey, I think they dream of a circle about this big. And on that circle, is a smaller circle, about two inches and a little darker in color. Sticking out from that smaller circle is a little sausage looking 'thingie' squirting luscious, nutritious pure white milk. I think they dream of milky boobs."

She stared at me for about three seconds with her mouth open. I stared back waiting for it. Then, we both burst out laughing.

Other than the biological boob and womb differences between genders, I believe men and women are equal in their ability to raise daughters or sons. Just because there is history on anything, that does not mean it is applicable today.

I differ from my ancestors. I don't spend all day chopping down trees for building materials and warmth or hunting bison while my family stays home. *I am pretty sure I would suck at hunting bison.*

It wasn't long ago when women were not allowed to vote or people were legally owned as slaves in our country.

There are a lot of examples like this. History teaches us unequal rights, oppression and slavery are wrong. Most importantly, history teaches that change is possible.

We live in a different time. The traditional gender lines and parenting roles are disintegrating. More women are working, and more fathers are willing to raise their children.

It is becoming more acceptable for men to wear pink and women to "wear the pants" in the family. Do we still have a way to go?

"Yes, but change occurs only when it is demanded. Fathers must insist society support our active participation in the lives of our children."

Today, I can proudly name all the ponies and princesses. I know all about pets in little pet shops, and those that live in palaces. I woke up many times with as many as four mermaid dolls snoozing on the pillow next to me.

From the childhood days of my oldest daughter, I know that La La the Teletubbie spells her name "Laa-Laa," and that she is yellow and talks in a baby voice. And, I still know all the words and melody to the hit song "Hot Potato" by The Wiggles, one of her favorites.

> Hot Potato, Hot Potato
> Hot Potato, Hot Potato
> Hot Potato, Hot Potato
> Potato, Potato, Potato, Potato

See? Pretty impressive, I know.

My oldest daughter and I rarely share conversations about Laa-Laa or The Wiggles anymore, but we still share. We now talk about big girl stuff.

We talk about ideals, fears, and desires. We play, listen to and talk about music together. We watch interesting shows that are too grown-up for my other daughters, and talk about them afterwards.

We talk about money, God, history, and science, just about anything.

My middle daughter is a bit more encompassing of today's pop-culture characters. She digs ponies but is also fond of superheroes: Thor, Iron Man, Spiderman, Hulk and many of Stan Lee's other marvelous characters. She also likes Batman (DC), but just slightly more than she likes Twilight Sparkle from My Little Pony.

My little one likes to paint my nails. But, she also likes to hunt imaginary zombies with a gun that shoots harmless, foamy bullets.

She thinks I am a great host of tea parties. I understand American Girl and even though it took a while, I now totally relate to the Shopkins.

Speaking of shopping, I shop for any and every one of my daughter's needs, if you know what I mean.

I am engaged with my daughters' doctors, teachers, and parents of their friends. I help heal their heartaches. We work through challenges that arise in their social sphere. We discuss the message portrayed in the clothes they wear. *Fixing their hair is the one skill I never mastered, but I get by. I have sold my girls on the "natural" look.*

We color with crayons. We paint. We play music together. We play Hide and Go Seek. We play with a variety of dolls. We play, we play and we play. And sometimes we laugh, and sometimes we cry. *For the record, I am very sure that I have cried at more Pixar movies than all my daughters combined.*

I teach my girls to listen to their inner voice, be aware of their feelings, and choose their thoughts. Above all, I teach them to love themselves. From the oldest to the youngest, they are empowered, full of self-respect, and believe in their own dreams.

Despite some of my "girlie" traits, I have retained my "boyish" ways, that I have shared with them as well. No, we don't kill cicadas. I share with them my "better boy" self, a refined person, a respectful "boy."

I love sports, lighting fireworks, driving go-carts at high speeds, watching my alma mater's sporting events, and playing video games. My girls have embraced these delights with the same intensity as they embraced princesses, flowers, and pink things.

Single moms have served in this dual role for years. There is no reason dads cannot do the same. Don't worry about not being trained. Your daughter will teach you everything you need to know to be her dad.

THE ELEPHANT IN THE ROOM... AND MOMS

Ok, first of all, let me tell you about the mothers of my daughters. There are two, and both are very special because they are the moms of some very amazing girls. They do not have big ears or long noses. They do not love peanuts and they do not trumpet when excited. Their skin is not gray and wrinkled (yet), and they do not measure their weight in tons.

I do laugh when I imagine their reaction upon reading the name of this chapter.

I am a single dad. The very fact that I am writing this chapter about elephants, is an indication that society is not quite ready for single dads stepping up in the primary role.

If this book was written by a single mom, about moms and their daughters or sons, only a few would ask "What is the deal with dad?" But I am pretty sure that most females reading this book are asking "What is the deal with mom?" There is nothing wrong with either mom.

There is nothing 'wrong' with anyone for that matter.

My girls living with me is the best situation for them. The truth is, usually one parent is going to be in a better position to provide for their children.

The decision for the primary parent, needs to be made for the sake of the child or children and only for that reason. If it is dad, then he needs to be willing to take that step and moms need to be willing to let it happen.

I want to leave this chapter, because elephants are big and they hurt your feet when they step on you. Here are my final thoughts.

Be involved, very involved in your child's life. It matters a lot. It is the gift that keeps on giving. And, finally, have as healthy a relationship as possible with your co-parent. From one who knows, it is possible even in the most unlikely situations.

That does not mean you are "BFFs." Heck, your co-parent might very well hate your guts. Even in that case, you can still have a healthy relationship. Notice I said "you." I did not say "the two of you." *You* do it, for the sake of your children.

PART 2

My Daughter, You Woke Me Up

A PRAYER YOU MIGHT HAVE PRAYED

My dear darling daughter, right before you were born, I imagine you could have said a prayer like the one below.

"Dear God, it is almost my time, but maybe we can talk about this a little more before it happens. Don't get me wrong. I'm fired up and ready to be born. Seeing all those little drooling, chunky babies bubbling over with happiness, I can hardly wait to say 'Goo goo, gaa gaa!'

"Those babies are soaring high with joy! They love every second of their new life and can hardly wait to experience the next moment. But then, babies grow older. They no longer drool, but that is probably a good thing. They no longer bubble with happiness, and that does not seem like a good thing. Their excitement for that next moment is replaced with dread, fear, and worry. 'Why God, why?'

"It is interesting that babies are so happy. They can't do very much on their own. They can't do that walking thing or choose what to eat or what to wear.

"I mean seriously, have you seen some of those outfits parents put on babies?

"Then, in the blink of an eye, those babies grow up to be kids. Kids know how to do all kinds of things. Kids can run, walk and skip. Kids get to have opinions about food, clothes, music and all kinds of stuff. Kids get to make lots of choices. Being a kid should 'Rock!' The fun should only get 'funner,' right? But it doesn't. Why not?

"Then those kids become adults. 'Yikes!' This is where things really get scary. Adults know how to do even more stuff than kids. But, they don't seem to have any fun at all. They honk their horns, talk bad about others, tap their foot when things take too long, shout, have bad manners, lie, steal, hit, say mean things, give dirty looks and fight. 'Yuck, yuckity, yuckiest!'

"And OMG, the worrying! What is the deal with the worrying? Those adults worry about everything. Seriously, just look at my dad, waiting for me to be born. As an adult, he can do anything he wants, but he spends most of his time worrying. He goes to bed worrying, wakes up worrying, worries all day and even worries in his dreams. He hardly smiles.

"God, I know you did not intend for this gift of life to start all bubbly and then go flat.

"I know, I know. It is time for me to be born. Hey God, do me a favor. Show me how I can have the kind of life You meant for all of us to have. You know, the kind of life that keeps getting better.

"But, if my life starts feeling more 'yucky' than fun, then please bring me back home. That will probably be around the time I start high school. From what I can tell, that is when things really get sucky.

"Ok Daddy-o, let's do this. Let me be born."

MY AWAKENING

My darling daughter, you were born into a life intended to be full of love, happiness and fun. How do I know this? You showed me.

Within a few short weeks of your birth, you smiled. Of course, you did other things too, like crying, pooping, farting, drooling, peeing, sleeping, sucking, and eating.

But, that smiling thing was very different than the smelly, wet stuff that had a biological purpose. Your smile had no purpose. It just happened because you felt really, really good.

And what did I do? I exploded with joy. I bawled happy tears. And for a moment, I felt what you were feeling. I felt pure joy. Nothing else mattered at that moment. I was zapped by the immense power of a Superhero in the form of a little baby girl.

"Smiles are just that powerful!"

By the way, that crying thing you did then was not because you were sad. You arrived into this world fluent in the universally understood and fantastic language of "Waa! Waa!"

You see, crying was your way of letting me know you had an unfulfilled need. *Hungry? You cried. Sick? You cried. Feeling cold or too warm? You cried. In pain? You cried! Dirty diaper? You cried and you were also very stinky. Sleepy? Yooooou cried! In need of a loving touch? Heck yes, you cried. Touch is also a very important need my daughter.* You cried as a way to express need.

Now, here is something extremely cool. Depending on how serious your situation or specific need, your crying sounded different. Your "hungry cry" was very unique compared to your "sick cry." You also had an "urgent cry." "Hey, this is really serious and you need to come now!" That desperate sound can wake up the dead.

One time, at 3 AM, you woke me from a deep sleep with one of those urgent cries. *Before you were born, it was impossible to awaken me once I fell asleep. Now, it is almost impossible for me to remain sleeping if I hear the sound of your voice.*

When I went to your crib that morning at 3 AM, I discovered you had thrown up all over the place. Your fever was soaring. I don't even want to think about what might have happened if you had been left alone for another four hours.

Now, where was I? Oh yes, your first smile.

So, there I was, overwhelmed with joy after seeing you smile for the first time. I cried happy tears. Nothing else mattered.

Your smile made me feel the same way that you were feeling! But then, that joyful feeling departed. As quickly as that feeling came, it left. And this got me thinking.

You were born with joy. I was too. But, as I grew older, the less joyful I became.

Eventually, I completely forgot this birth knowledge. My life became very yucky and messy, kind of like stepping in "dog poop." I tracked gooey, smelly brown poop everywhere. Yes, just like that. A messy and stinky life became normal.

But, raising you changed me. The twinkle in your smiling eyes and your passion for living was vaguely recognizable, and that was enough to ignite a spark within me.

I slowly started to remember. And the more I remembered, the more I remembered, until one day...

I remembered, remembered, remembered!

On that day, my heart roared and screamed and cussed. "Why the #$@&%*! did I forget how life was meant to be? How can I get it back? And what in the h-e-double-toothpicks is that awful smell? Barf!"

You see my daughter, as I grew older, I had some experiences that didn't feel very good. I responded to those experiences by forming some "stinking thinking" habits. I started putting conditions on my life, dropping "if bombs" every few steps I took.

"*If* those people will just do what I want, then I will be happy."

"I would be happy *if* that had not happened."

"*If* what I want comes true, then I will be happy."

"*If* I get this 'thingamabob,' then I will be happy."

"*If* I can make that person happy, then I will be happy."

"*If* this, *if* that!"

A seeking heart will always find answers! Mine was definitely on the hunt, and I was desperate for answers so that I could find my way back home! Over the next several years, the answers came, seven to be exact. Each answer was a key that unlocked a heavy chain that I unknowingly carried around my neck.

Slowly but surely, I was able to identify the "stinking thinking" habits I had formed. With a little effort, I replaced those bad habits with good ones based on the truth I learned from you and your sisters. One by one, the chains fell off. Little by little, my life starting feeling better.

Before I knew it, life was wonderful. I stopped dropping "if bombs." There was no more stinky, smelly "doggie-poop" in my life.

This book is my gift to you for the gift you gave me. It is a collection of valuable keys to happiness, shared in seven chapters. They will help you rediscover what's most important in your life. I wanted to write them down for you, just in case you drift away from that happy, loving, and fun life you knew when you were born.

My hope is that by sharing this with you, you might not stink your life up too much or for too long, a day here or there instead of years. Heck, you might not stink your life up at all! But, if you do, that is okay. You are loved just the same. When you're ready to leave that stink and mess behind, this book will help you find your way back to happiness.

You see my daughters; your life is built from your thoughts and emotions. "Think good thoughts, feel that joy and you will have a good life. If you think bad thoughts and feel 'yucky,' you will have a rough life."

Your happiness depends on your thoughts, feelings, and attitude for life, "Nothing else!" If you think your happiness depends on what you have or what you experience, you will be grounded for dropping "if bombs," grounded by yourself, not by me.

It's really like a cake. Your happiness is the cake. The experiences you passionately pursue are the frosting and candles. Without the cake, you can't have the frosting and candles. Said another way, "Think good thoughts and feel happiness now, no matter what! That is how you felt when you were an infant."

Remember?

Then, appreciate the experiences that come your way. So, bake the cake (feel happiness) and spread the frosting. Apply the candles (go for it). Have a party every day (feel appreciation).

One last thing, "As your dad, I am going to do my very best to encourage you to choose the desires and experiences you feel are right for you. It is your life after all, not mine." The only way you can be passionate and have faith in what you desire, is if they are *your* desires and daydreams, not mine for you.

I might be better at this on some days than on others, but I know in my heart that choosing your own way is a requirement for happiness, both of ours. So on those days when I am having a hard time letting you make your own choices, don't fret. I will get back on track. I know the truth regarding happiness, and I'm not forgetting it ever again. Thank you for choosing me as your dad and becoming my child. I love you infinitely, which means without end and forever.

Love,

Dad

PART 3

Seven Keys to Happiness

KEY 1

Living With Naysayers

- Michelangelo was a Body Snatcher
- Dear Daughter, Don't Listen to "Naysayers"

This is the ceiling of the Sistine Chapel, located in Italy. An artist named Michelangelo painted this more than 500 years ago.

We can learn a lot from Michelangelo about living with Naysayers.

MICHELANGELO WAS A BODY SNATCHER

About 500 years ago, an artist named Michelangelo finished painting a masterpiece on the Sistine Chapel ceiling. His most famous painting on that ceiling is *Creation of Adam.*

The Sistine Chapel is in Italy. This country has a really fun shape. It looks like a boot. Can you see the resemblance?

Are we really surprised the Italians are the kings and queens of leather footwear fashion?

Michelangelo's painting *Creation of Adam* shows God and other heavenly beings on the right, and Adam on the left. God and Adam are touching fingers. This painting is just one of many that are on the ceiling.

The Sistine Chapel ceiling is rather large for an artistic painting. It is a rectangle about 40 by 13 steps (about 120 feet by 39 feet). *If you look at the image a few pages back you can almost see the entire ceiling, and you can see Creation of Adam near the top of the picture.*

The complete painting of the chapel took Michelangelo about four years to complete. This probably is due to the size and the fact he painted much of this work on the ceiling.

Can you imagine how hard that must have been to paint such large images on a ceiling? I bet he had to paint looking up while lying on his back. If he wanted to see what he painted, he had to climb down to the ground.

I am sure he needed a massage or two every week, since he looked up all the time. That had to hurt after a while.

Now where was I? Oh yes, In the early 1500's, when Michelangelo was finishing *Creation of Adam*, people were told what to believe about God by a few, very powerful individuals.

If anyone disagreed, they could get in serious trouble. I'm not talking about just a little trouble. Sometimes, people were beaten, stabbed, burned or even killed by those who made the rules. Many individuals who had alternate beliefs about God in those days, had to keep those thoughts to themselves. This was especially true for scientists, whose primary focus was to unravel the mysteries of God's wondrous creation.

As an example, you know the sun is at the center of our solar system. The planets Mercury, Venus, Earth, Mars, and the rest of the gang orbit around the sun.

And most of our planets in our solar system have one or more moons orbiting around them. Jupiter and Saturn have more than 60!

I don't know if you know this, but the twinkling stars you see in the sky at night are also suns! Many of those suns have planets orbiting around them. That's a lot of suns and planets. In fact, there are more suns in the universe than there are grains of sand on all the beaches in the world.

When Michelangelo was painting the Sistine Chapel, people believed Earth was the center of the entire universe and everything else orbited around it. All the planets, including our sun, moon and all the twinkling stars circled a motionless Earth. Earth was the center of the entire universe!

A guy named Copernicus discovered that the sun is the center of our solar system, not Earth. He lived around the same time as Michelangelo.

To give you an example of how scared these scientists were, Copernicus did not want his discovery shared with the world until after he died. He was afraid of being tortured or killed. He concealed his discovery for many years. It was not until after his death that his discoveries were made known to the masses.

You know you can't hurt a dead guy, right?

Speaking of smart dead guys, Michelangelo also had a secret! Know what it is? He was more than just a famous artist. He was also a full-fledged scientist.

Michelangelo was especially interested in the human body. He studied the skin, muscles, heart, stomach, brain, bones and many internal body parts rarely seen except around Halloween or Dia de los Muertos (Day of the Dead).

When Michelangelo was about 17 years old, he paid body snatchers to steal dead bodies from the morgues and deliver them into his secret laboratory. Guess what he did with those dead bodies? He cut them open to study their inner parts and the way those parts connected together.

Obviously, he was very careful because he was never caught. *Sounds pretty gross, I know.*

Now, it is important for you to know that what Michelangelo was doing with dead bodies was definitely against the rules. His actions put his life in danger! Here's why.

First, taking a dead body destined for the grave was considered stealing, although I am not sure from whom. The person living in that body was no longer there. I am sure they did not care. Maybe it was considered stealing from the family, which is completely understandable.

Another rule Michelangelo broke was "Science is a NO-NO!" Studying how the body worked by cutting up the corpse of a dead person was definitely science.

This particular kind of science also broke some very specific religious rules that were in force at that time. All dead bodies were supposed to be laid to rest in a grave. Cutting dead bodies in to pieces was considered vandalizing something holy. Human bodies, dead or alive, were considered holy. Cutting dead bodies in to pieces was like spitting in the face of God.

Did you know that in our country today, any person that is legally considered an adult can donate their body to science after they die? Now what do you think will happen to their body? Most likely, it will get the Michelangelo treatment. It will be cut apart and studied.

I want to go off on a tangent here and talk about religious laws. These are just my thoughts. Ok? My initial reaction to some of the old religious laws is that they are just silly and misplaced for people living today. But then I take a step back and think about the time in which they were written, and from that perspective some of those laws make a lot of sense.

Around 3,000 years ago, some spiritual laws were written in the Old Testament that forbid touching of dead bodies, except in very specific cases.

3,000 years ago, people did not know there was a microscopic world full of germs that could make people sick or die if certain precautions were not followed. In fact, even during Michelangelo's lifetime, they still did not know about microbes.

These spiritual laws guided people in times of sorrow, when their thinking might lead them to do things that could be harmful, like kissing a dead loved one or keeping them around too long. You see, when people are grieving, they don't always think clearly.

To give this even more context, there were also spiritual laws that forbid the eating of pork, shrimp and some other stuff that many of us eat today. Yep! Bacon is pork. Wonderful bacon was a "No! No!"

You must remember that there were no refrigerators in those times. Those specific foods spoiled fast at room temperature. And spoiled pork and shrimp is loaded with microorganisms that can make you very sick.

Since people did not know about microbes back then, it was important to guide them to safe food choices. Obviously, the explanation could not be about microbes since no one knew about microbes. The only explanation that made sense and would be followed was a religious one.

Honestly, those spiritual laws were very good during those times, when there were no fridges or knowledge of the microscopic world. Today, Science has answered many questions about microorganisms. We have developed ways to make food safe. Today, those forbidden foods are commonly consumed.

Ok, tangent over. Again, these are just my thoughts, so take them with a grain of salt. Let's get back to Michelangelo's time. ✦

Now why do you think that science was such a "no-no" to the people that made the religious rules during the time that Michelangelo lived? You see, the rule-makers believed that when any facet of God's creation was explained by science, God's greatness took a hit. Explained miracles were no longer miraculous. *This type of thinking is still happening today in some parts of the world.*

Weird, right?

Let me tell you something, "The more we understand, the less we actually know. As soon as we answer one question, two unanswered questions of 'how' and 'why' always come next."

Personally, the more I learn about the way things work, the more awestruck I become about the Creator and Creation. I always think, "Wow, what an amazing design." But, as I said, that was not the case when Michelangelo was alive. Those "How?" and "Why?" questions were "No Bueno!"

I have a hunch that Michelangelo knew about germs. As far as we know, he never became deathly ill while he was cutting up the dead, rotting bodies that were playing host to the latest microbes "rave party." Obviously, he did something to keep himself safe.

Now, fast forward with me 16 years after Michelangelo was body snatching, and I will show you something quite astounding. *Let's see, he was 17 years old when he was body snatching, so 16 years later Michelangelo would have been how old? Correct, 33.*

When Michelangelo was around 33 years old, he started painting on the ceiling of the Sistine Chapel. Though we do not know specifically what Michelangelo believed, his painting *Creation of Adam* reveals he had some knowledge about the human body, and perhaps some thoughts about how we were created and our connection to God.

Of course, he could not share these thoughts openly. Take a look at the right side of *Creation of Adam*, the God-side, with something superimposed on top.

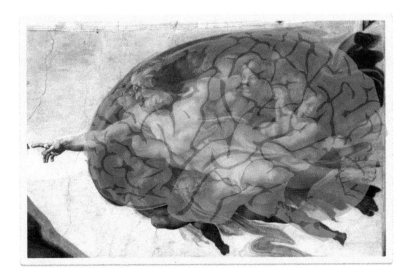

"OMG!" How cool is that? How do you think Michelangelo knew the shape of a brain? Remember those body snatchers? He probably held a brain in his hands like a pirate holding his treasure when he scores his booty!

Though we can't be sure of Michelangelo's exact thoughts, clearly he believed that the brain or the mind played a part in our creation and our connection to God. The "rule-makers" would have been very angry if they knew he hid such an idea on the ceiling of a church, and got paid for doing it. Pretty cool stuff, huh?

There are some "naysayers" that might challenge this connection between Michelangelo's art and his discoveries in science, using their favorite "c word," coincidence. Sometimes you have to use that thing in the picture above, your brain. It looks pretty obvious to me. Does it to you?

Naysayers are like the darkness of space. Without them, we could not see you shine like the stars above.

DEAR DAUGHTER, DON'T BELIEVE NAYSAYERS

Dear Daughter,

You are surrounded by "naysayers." Michelangelo was too. There have always been naysayers. There will always be naysayers.

This is going to sound weird, but naysayers can be a healthy and helpful part of your development. They can help you shape your ideas. They can get your creative juices flowing and inspire you. Some days, they will make you mad as heck, and that is OK.

On the other hand, naysayers can also kill your dreams and urge you to feel hopeless. Dream killing and hope stealing are not healthy or helpful at all.

I have good news my daughter. Learning how to live with naysayers in a healthy and happy way is easy, and I can tell you how to do it!

First, you have to be able to spot them. Naysayers are all about limitations. They use words like: "can't," "don't," "shouldn't" and other negative words.

You can also add "if" to the list.

Naysayers are not butt heads, but they are also very good at using the word "but." I know I used the word "but" in the middle of that last sentence, but that is not the kind of "but" usage I am talking about.

Man, that is a lot of buts.

I am talking about this kind of "but."

You say, "Hey, I have this great idea. We could blah, blah, (*insert great idea details*), blah, blah, blah." And then the naysayer says, "But... blah, blah, blah (*insert reason why great idea will not work*), blah, blah, blah."

Yikes, that is one ugly but.

Here is a list of other common naysayer statements.

"You can't because you are a girl."

"You can't because you are not the right age."

"You can't because you are not educated."

"You can't because you are not the right size."

"You can't because you are not fast enough."

"You can't because you are not strong enough."

"You can't because you are not the right skin color."

"You can't because you are not rich enough."

"You can't because you do not speak the right language."

"You can't because you are not 'normal.'"

"You can't because you are not from here."

"You can't because you are not popular."

"You can't because you are handicapped or disabled."

And if none of those fit, there is always the "trump card statement" used in Michelangelo's time, and still used today.

"You can't because God says you can't."

Give me a minute, I need to vomit.

Listen!!! The greatest stories of individuals are in fact stories that proved the naysayers wrong. For every "you can't" listed above, there are gobs of examples from history and even today that showed otherwise.

Identifying naysayers is piece of cake. I mean, they are everywhere. They use the same negative words over and over and over and over. Their favorite word is "can't" in case you did not know.

Now you know how to identify naysayers. What now? "What's a girl to do, living amongst all of these naysayers?"

Love, I am so glad you asked that question. Let's first talk about day-to-day survival tips.

It is impossible to stop naysayers from believing what they believe or saying what they say! So, don't even try. I mean that. "No way Jose." You can't do it. Say it out loud. "I cannot control others." Say it like you mean it. "I CANNOT CONTROL OTHERS." Ok, do you believe you?

Know that the only person you *can* control is you.

This is soooooo important.

Pretty please, say with me, "I *can* control me. I *can* choose my thoughts."

Ready?

"I CAN CONTROL ME. I CAN CHOOSE MY THOUGHTS."

Do you believe you?

There is no way to avoid hearing the message of naysayers. But, you don't have to listen. *There is a big difference between hearing and listening.*

Right?

Do however, listen to messages that are uplifting and encouraging. This includes what you "listen" to with your eyes. These messages will not come from naysayers. They come from believers. *You do know the difference between believer and naysayer messages.*

Right?

Choose friends that are mostly encouraging and uplifting. Nobody is perfect, which is why I said "mostly." Isn't it more fun to be around these uplifting friends anyway?

Stay away from naysayers on social media, the internet, TV and the movies. Throw music in there too.

I mean, you don't eat trash out of dumpsters. Don't feed your mind trash either. You are what you eat and absorb.

True?

Some days it will be easy to believe in you, but there will be days when you experience doubt. There will also be days that are just funky, and everything is out of sorts. On those doubting or funky days, be more private.

Those days will pass faster than you think. Doesn't the sun always come up after a dark night?

Count your blessings always! Even during your most difficult times. You have more blessings than you can count at any given moment.

Do you know this?

Of course, if you need to share during those difficult times, do so with someone that is an "uplifter."

Tweeting (or re-tweeting) "Life is nothing but a string of broken dreams!" is the worst action you could take. That is like lighting a grassfire. *You know that fires are dangerous.*

Right?

And finally, the simplest, yet most important tip of all. Practice every single day, being a believer. It only takes a few moments every day.

When you first wake up, spend a few moments in your bed imagining how wonderful the day is going to be.

"I feel great about today."

"Today is going to be full of wonderful happenings."

"My mind is going to be sharp."

"I am going to have fun."

"I am going to be relaxed during my test."

"I am going to buzz with energy."

"Something is going to make me laugh, I can't wait to see what it is going to be."

"I am going to have some great ideas today."

As you are falling asleep, spend a few moments in your bed expressing gratitude for the wonderful experiences you had that day. Tell yourself that your sleep is going to be great, and that you hope to have a really fun dream.

Naysayers provide a constant "drone of negativity and limitations." If you don't counter that on a daily basis, you will find yourself getting comfortable with that "drone." You will also find yourself acting like a naysayer more than usual. "Yuck."

My lovely daughter, you were born with a creative, loving and believing spirit. That spirit is in your DNA. It is who you are.

Look around you! Have you noticed that everything that exists is expanding? Cells divide, flowers make more plants which make more flowers. Viruses evolve. New stars are being made in the universe at this very moment. Galaxies, people, trees, amoebas; everything is expanding. From the biggest to the smallest, this is true.

The created, creates.

Now, here is where it gets interesting. Every creative process is coupled with some form of resistance.

I mean, is the word "labor" not the most perfect description for childbirth? Just ask your mom what that was like.

When I was little, I watched for many days the process of a butterfly emerging from a chrysalis. It was painfully 'slooooow,' like watching paint dry. I wanted to cut it open.

I would like to tell you that I wanted to help. That butterfly was having to work so hard. But that would not be true. I was a normal boy.

Remember?

I wanted to cut it open to get it over with. I mean, "Come on butterfly, how many days is this going to last?"

My dad told me that if I cut open the chrysalis, the butterfly would not be a butterfly. Lots of stuff happens inside that chrysalis and during the exit. What looks like struggle, is in fact necessary.

That squeezing process pumps body fluid and insect blood to the wings, which causes them to expand. In a way, naysayers are the chrysalis for believers. They inspire and strengthen us to transform, to be more.

The last point I want to share with you is about timing. You are going to experience flashes of brilliance throughout your life. When you do, take some time to let that brilliant flash of genius germinate in your mind before you share with others. How long it takes, is up to you. It could be minutes, days, or longer.

Just let your flash of genius have time to get its roots planted. If you blurt out your brilliant thought without roots, a naysayer can easily snatch it from you with just a few choice words.

Although Michelangelo's naysayers were far more dangerous than the naysayers you encounter, the strategy he used is the same for you. Know when it is the right time to bring forth your flash of inspiration, and be choosey with whom you share it with. And remember, there is only one person that has to believe in you my Love, and that person is YOU.

Sweetheart, I want to always be the type of father that is a believer. I know that I have at times acted like a naysayer, and I might have even squashed a dream or two that you shared. If so, I am truly sorry. Some days I might be better at this than on other days, but I know in my heart that being a believer is best for me and you.

Love,

Dad

KEY 2

Living in a Zombie Apocalypse

- The Modern Zombie
- Dear Daughter, Dead Things Stink for a Reason

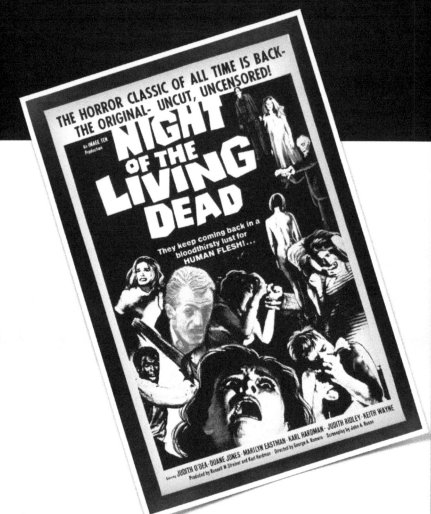

This is the movie poster from George A. Romero's horror masterpiece Night of the Living Dead, written in 1968. This movie defined what we believe about zombies today.

Zombies can teach us so much about life, and how to stay alive while living it.

THE MODERN ZOMBIE

In the last chapter about Michelangelo, you learned how dead people gave life to his creativity. Recall that when he was 17 years old, he paid to have dead bodies snatched from the morgue, before they were buried in their graves. He had the dead bodies delivered in the dark of night, to his laboratory where he studied the human body pieces and parts, up close and personal.

This seems like the perfect time to talk about the pop-culture kings and queens of the macabre. They are the living dead. "Everybody, please give a warm welcome to the ZOMBIES!"

Zombies are very alive in our culture! I am no horror expert, but it is pretty obvious zombies are by far the most popular nightmare character today.

I mean seriously, vampires suck.

Werewolves are nothing but "rare wolves." "Hey wolfie. If you want to be top dog in Monster Town, you have to come around more than once every 29 days." *Did you know that a full moon comes only once every 29 days?*

Werewolves and vampires don't stand a chance against the never sleeping, always eating, zombie.

All puns aside, I do find it odd that zombies are the most popular monsters. I mean, vampires are so suave and sophisticated. They are those "tall, dark and handsome monsters."

Werewolves have that mystical quality. They are one with nature in body and spirit. And, just like real wolves, werewolves are social. They look out for one another, like a family. You "gotta" love that.

Zombies? I can't think of a single zombie characteristic or quality that is redeeming or inviting. They stink. They are ugly. And they have terrible manners when they eat.

Why Zombie, why? Why are you so popular?

The history of zombie lore goes back a long way, thousands of years in fact. But, the zombie that you know, love and hate was created by motion pictures beginning in the late 1960's.

Now that I think about it, much of what you believe is influenced by motion pictures. "Gosh, I wonder if those movie makers realize just how much influence they have on us?" Maybe a better question to ask is, "I wonder if you realize how influential they are?"

The modern zombie was introduced to the world in two movies directed by George A. Romero. The first movie, *Dawn of the Dead* was released in 1968. The second one, *Night of the Living Dead* hit the big-screen in 1978.

These two movies started the salvo that led to the popularity of zombies today and cemented their place as the victor among monsters.

They also defined the plot of zombie films and the characteristics of the (mostly) nameless zombies that are featured in the majority of zombie movies produced in the last 30 years.

Why zombie, why? Why are you so popular?

Your Dad's first zombie movie was Romero's *Night of the Living Dead*. This movie was very disturbing for me. Even though I was almost old enough to drive a car, I watched a good chunk of that movie peeking between my fingers. Afterwards, I wondered about my friends.

Why friends, why? Why did I let you pressure me in to seeing this movie?

Let's take a look at the plot of zombie films. If you have seen one zombie movie, you have seen nearly all of them.

Early in the films, the dead are brought back to life. Usually, they pop out of the ground like fast growing corn.

The reason the zombies came to life in *Night of the Living Dead* was never really explained.

Later films blamed magic, scientists-gone-bad, radiation, a virus or "extra terrestrials." The cause is not really important to the plot. What happens next is.

After the dead come back to life, they hunt for living people to eat! Evidently, zombies are really hungry. You rarely see them doing anything else but eat. You don't see them talking to their kids about their day. You don't see them sitting in a rocking chair at night, gazing at the stars and thinking deep thoughts. They just eat!

The living humans don't really like being eaten. *That makes sense.*

Right?

So, they respond by waging war against the zombies. The end game is zombie extinction. Take no prisoners. Kill or be killed. It is an all-out war with only one acceptable end.

No more zombies.

Zombie plots also contain some personal, emotional crisis. Typically, there is at least one zombie who had a special "love" relationship with a still-living person, before becoming a zombie. By special, I mean they were a parent, child, brother or sister, best friend or someone they loved romantically. Of course, the living person is horrified by their loved one's transformation into a zombie.

You see where this is going.

Right?

I think I said this back in the chapter about Michelangelo, "People don't always think clearly when they experience the loss of a loved one."

Somehow, someway the living family member or lover and the zombie, meet. The living person feels all kinds of emotions for their lost loved one. I get it. I probably would too.

Thank goodness zombies are not real. Or are they?

The zombie on the other hand, feels nothing emotional when they meet. Instead, the zombie thinks meat.

The living person just knows that the zombie will remember the love they once shared together.

Nope! No remembering.

The living person puts themselves in a dangerous situation, like staring into the eyes of the zombie to reignite the love spark.

Nope! No spark.

The living person gets eaten.

Yep!

Now tell me, does that plot sound familiar? Isn't this just like every zombie film you have seen?

That is a trick question. If you say yes, then I have to ask, "Have you seen a zombie film without my knowledge?"

Hmmm!

Now that we have covered the plot of zombie films, let's take a quick look at the characteristics of zombies. Today's zombies are very similar to Romero's zombies, except the more recent ones run really fast.

"Pa-lease." A fast zombie? Hello? Rigor mortis? Those are not zombies.

Ok, let me tell you truth about rigor mortis. Within a few hours after death, the process of rigor mortis kicks in and the body gets stiff. This stiffness lasts for about 3 days. After that, the stiffness goes away. In the zombie movies I am talking about here, the zombies remained stiff from rigor mortis.

Let's take a look at the characteristics of zombies. It is really important that you recognize a zombie, just in case you cross paths with one.

Obviously, if you know someone that has died, and you see them moving around at the mall, "Run!" That is obviously a zombie. But how do you spot a zombie when you didn't know their living version? Here is how.

Zombies speak in a language that is nothing like they used to speak. Maybe other zombies can understand this language, but to living people like us, it sounds like a bunch of moaning.

Zombies are hungry all the time, no matter how much they eat. And what is it that zombies eat exactly? They are particularly fond of living human's brains. You know, the brain, the blobby thing Michelangelo hid in his painting *Creation of Adam*. You use it for making decisions and stuff.

Zombies make more zombies. Like everything else that exists, zombies expand. Zombies turn living people into zombies by sinking their teeth into them.

Listen love, zombies are dangerous! It only takes one to make a bunch of zombies. Zombies are dead and you are alive. Don't hang out with zombies.

Zombies are slow, I mean really slow, rigor mortis slow. A living person like you should have no problem staying away from a zombie. You are fast, alert, smart and agile. Zombies are not.

Yet, despite this great advantage, zombies seem to have no problem catching their next meal. Zombies are persistent. They never give up.

Crud, that story of the "Tortoise and the Hare" just popped into my head. I guess success is not all about ability. If ability was more important than persistence and determination, the tortoise would have never won that race. Persistence and a "never-quit attitude" must play a part in success.

Zombies are very unhealthy. Their skin is tinted gray and full of holes. Parts of their flesh are falling off. They have raccoon-like eyes that are all sunken in. They look like they haven't eaten a good meal in weeks. Zombie bodies are all tense and tight from rigor mortis. In other words, stiff.

Zombies are ugly. If Miss America became a zombie, even she would be ugly.

I have never heard a living person say, "Whoa, do you see that zombie, the one on the right with the holes in her cheeks? Not that one, that one. See the one walking all tense and slow with the broken neck and that lovely moaning voice? Hubba hubba!"

Why zombie, why? Why are you so popular?

It just so happens that sociologists and social anthropologists have attempted to answer my "Why zombie, why?" question. You won't believe some of their explanations.

Ahem, ahem! Excuse me for a second. Ahem. I am changing my voice to sound stuffy and all educated. Ahem. Ok, got it.

"The zombie phenomenon is the result of our increasingly complex society. Global warming and wild animals becoming more domesticated and thus confused, also contribute to the phenomenon. Even elementary schools contribute. Many of these schools no longer serve fish on Fridays due to the ever increasing number of students receiving free lunches. The cost of fish is just too expensive."

Ok, I made that up. But seriously, there are some goofy theories.

The real explanations offered by these "smartie pants" include: politics, certain presidents, war, drugs, the war on drugs, inequality, technology, and more things that I am very sure you and other young girls and boys think about every day. This explains why zombie costumes are so popular on Halloween for children under 13.

Phooey, followed by a raspberry sound as my vibrating tongue sprays spit all over the place.

Listen, I am open to the hidden connection concept in pop culture offered by those PhD's. But, I am a DAD, and my common-sense meter tells me that those explanations are ridiculous.

Here is some advice for you. Smart sounding people are very effective at getting others to believe what they are saying, even when they are selling piles of poop.

Hitler was smart and charismatic. Many believed the poop he sold was as good as gold.

Listen to what is being said! It is more important than who is saying it. Check your heart and gut. If you can strip away all the external influences, your heart and gut will sniff out the "B.S."

One of the coolest things about your life is that you get to choose how you feel about everything. It is your birthright. So, allow me to exercise my birthright. I have a theory that explains why zombies are so popular.

Zombies represent something that is potentially very destructive to everyone! And the older each of us becomes, the more vulnerable we are! Give me a drumroll, for I am about to enlighten the world as to the cause of the zombie phenomenon.

Excuse me for a second. Ahem. I am changing my voice to sound stuffy and all educated. Ahem. Ok, got it.

"Zombies represent each person's past."

Nailed it!

The past events in your life are like dead bodies in a graveyard. They cannot be brought back to life. Those events can never be changed.

Some of those moments from your past felt very good, but some did not. If you spend too much time reliving the painful events of the past, the dead memories come alive. You feel just like you did when those painful events occurred. You experience the pain all over, again.

You don't keep scratching off your scabs when they form over you skinned knees, do you? Eventually, your wound will heal, but the pain and time to heal will be greater than it would have been if you had just kept it clean, protected it, and left it alone. You will also have a bigger scar.

It is no different when you relive painful moments from the past. In a sense, you are ripping off the scab, making the healing process take much longer. And you will have an emotional scar that will always be there to remind you.

I know I told you that zombies are not real, but in a way, they are. I have seen them. You have too. Let's take a closer look.

Have ever known someone that got stuck on some hurtful event from their past? By stuck, I mean stuck; like stuck in the mud, stuck for months or years on that hurt. They talk about it all the time. They think about it all the time.

I know some 40 year-olds that are still talking about something that happened when they were 10 years old. Thinking about this past pain becomes as much of a part of their life as taking a poop. Gross, I know. It is gross.

It is not uncommon for this type of person to blame others for their misfortune. A person like this takes no responsibility for their actions. Because of this, they are not able to heal and move on with their lives.

Even though these people were born brilliant like the rest of us, when they are in this state, their mind is gone. They are the last person you would trust with anything important. They can't think clearly or make good decisions. They traded their brains for spaghetti. These people are zombies.

Have you ever known someone that was full of regret? Despite the fact that they should have no regrets about anything, they discard that wisdom and think over and over about something they wish they had not done.

It's almost as if they believe they can change the past.

Guess what, they can't.

They say over and over, "If only I had not done that, my life would be so much better and full of hope." You and I call this moaning. These people are zombies.

Have you ever known anyone that was a scorekeeper? They keep track of all the supposed wrong things that people have done, even things that happened a long time ago.

Whenever anyone upsets this type of person, they quickly reach into their memory banks. They attempt to lay waste to that person, hoping to strike them in the heart with a painful reminder of their "failures" from the past.

They carry around all that baggage. That makes them very tense and stressed out. Their shoulders are lifted and their body becomes contorted. Just like rigor mortis.

Of course, they are also unhealthy due to the constant stress. *Did you know that stress is the biggest cause of poor health? Stress also makes a beautiful face, ugly.* These people are zombies.

Have you ever noticed that the people I just described, like to hang out with happy people? Why? Because they want to bring others down. These people are hungry to have their sad stories heard by those that don't tell sad stories.

They desperately want the happy people to have sympathy for them. They want them to know and even feel how they feel. They might even want to convince the happy people to take responsibility for making them feel better. They try to convince them that a true friend would make that sacrifice.

They don't purposely feed on happy people. They are just hungry for brains, and a happy brain is the tastiest. These people are zombies. My Love, when you come across zombies get away from them! You are smarter, faster and more beautiful, relaxed, articulate and healthier than those creeps.

But, don't write them off as hopeless. Unlike the Romero zombies, these zombies can return to a normal life.

Zombies are disgusting, stinky, sickly, stiff, slow, dumb... and they moan and groan all the time. They are also very dangerous.

What is dead should stay dead. When you relive painful memories over and over, you are giving life to the dead.

DEAR DAUGHTER, DEAD THINGS STINK FOR A REASON

Dear Daughter,

As soon as something dies, all kinds of crazy stuff happens. Shortly after a plant, animal or insect dies, a team of bacteria, fungi and worms come to an "all-you-can-eat-until-we-run-out-buffet."

When the buffet runs out of food, the dead creature is part of the soil. The whole process is actually quite beautiful.

But, we seldom see it that way. Dead things look scary. Rotting dead things smell just awful. That stuff can cause nightmares. It makes us blow chunks.

The microbe team of bacteria, fungi and worms are called "decomposers." Their feast is called decomposition.

When those little guys are feasting, and breaking down the dead body into soil, a lot of smelly gas is produced that stinks.

When you eat a hamburger, what comes out of you when you do a "Number 2" looks and smells nothing like a hamburger.

Thank goodness for that.

That hamburger was broken down by tiny bugs in your body during digestion. During the digestive process, stinky gas is produced. Oftentimes, the gas makes you fart.

Ha. I bet you smiled just now.

Well, when those decomposers are decomposing a dead thing, gas is also created. So in a way, the smell of decomposition is kind of like "BACTERIA FARTS."

Those farts aren't the kind that make you giggle, like you do with your own farts. Those farts, that decomposing smell, make you want to vomit.

And they don't even make the funny sounds that your farts make.

If you just so happened to eat something that is decomposing, the chances are very good that you will get sick. You may vomit or have the runs.

See? That "Number 2" not looking like a hamburger or smelling like one is a good thing.

In a way, the awful smell that occurs during decomposition is a warning sign to stay away. The potential sickness that might befall you is more than enough reason to be cautious.

Now, you must be wondering what on earth this is all about. Why am I telling you this? I am so glad you asked.

There are two very different aspects of life that exist together. On the one side, there is the physical realm. This is where you experience life using your senses of smell, taste, touch, sight and sound.

On the other side, there is the emotional and spiritual realm. This realm includes: thoughts, personality, emotions and feelings, memories, day and night dreams and wishes.

Of course experiences in one realm may impact the other. "Chocolate, yummy chocolate." Eat that stuff, and feel pure joy!

Though these two realms seem very different, the truths they each reveal are the same. In a sense, the physical is a reflection of the spiritual. And why wouldn't that be the case? I mean, think about it. The Creator and Source of everything is a spiritual force that created the physical universe.

You were born you, in the form of a person. That is the physical you. You were made from me and your mom, but you also have the genes of all your grandparents, and their parents, and their parents, and on and on it goes back to the very first mom and dad in your family line. Wow!

But bundled with the physical you is your spirit, or what some call your soul. So in a sense, you are two in one. *If you don't know what I mean by that, think about a robot. You can touch them, but they definitely do not have a spirit.*

Let me say right now to not get caught up in the "evolution versus creation" argument. It does not matter a flip, and has no impact on what I am telling you here. HOW the physical realm came into existence does not matter. THAT the physical realm came into existence, is all that matters.

Now here is where things get truly cool. You can find the answers to emotional and spiritual questions you may have, by observing the physical realm. And believe me, you will have lots of questions over the course of your life. If your eyes are open to the physical world and the way it works, you can find the answers.

Many of your questions will be about resolving painful experiences, and how to not repeat them again.

And that my Love, is why I am talking about all of this dead, stinking stuff. There is wisdom to discover.

When living things die, their previous physical form is gone. You cannot bring their dead parts back. Hopefully, you don't want to keep their dead bodies around. You can't bring them back to life. That cannot be changed.

If you could bring them back, they would be zombies, and zombies are not good.

When something dies, bacteria and the rest of "team microbe," amazing little guys that they are, do what they do best. They eat breakfast, lunch and dinner nonstop. That is how things work in the physical world.

The same is true for the emotional and spiritual realm, regarding past events. You cannot change the past or bring it back.

As soon as a painful moment occurs, "spiritual decomposers" get to work. As more time elapses, the impact of that moment fades away, just like a body that is decomposing. There is nothing you need to do to make this happen. It just does! It starts at the moment the experience ends.

That is how things work in the spiritual world. And though there is no stinky smell to keep you away, you do have your feelings.

Returning to something hurtful in your mind feels really bad. That is your warning to stay away. Those feelings stink.

So, what I am saying to you Love is this; "You cannot change the past. *You know this!* Learn from it. Definitely remember the wonderful times in the past."

At least once every day, I find myself smiling from ear to ear when I think of some memory I have of you. I smile even now while I am writing this.

There will be times in your life when some experience hurts a lot. It will take a little longer to work through that.

Working through it however, requires a very different type of energy than regretting or replaying it. So, invest your energy in accepting that whatever you are working through cannot be changed.

Find some type of appreciation for that experience. Do not resent others. Tell yourself it is going to be okay, because it is. I promise!

Know there are tiny little bugs – not really... but kind of – working fast and with great efficiency on that memory. They are breaking it down into nourishment for new experiences. Sometimes, you just need to relax and do nothing. Trust the process!

I know there will be times when you hurt really badly. If I know about it, I will also hurt for you. I can't help it.

Please know that your daddy has also been through hurtful times. No matter what, everything will be okay. Everything always turns out ok. The sun always comes up after darkness. Spring always comes after winter.

What I am sharing with you now, really works. It is natural, exactly as my own dad taught me.

Love,

Dad

KEY 3

Staying Out of the Dark

- Opposite Day
- Dear Daughter, You Cannot Want
  What You Do Not Want

Shadows are profound. They tickle our imagination, urging us on to fill in the details. Some of the time, we feel afraid. Some of the time, we laugh.

The nature of shadows and how they are made can teach us a lot about our thoughts.

OPPOSITE DAY

In the last chapter, we talked about zombies. Zombies are both dead and alive at the same time, and in fact are often called the "living dead." This seems like the perfect time to talk about opposites.

My mind was blown when I became aware of what I'm about to share with you. And just for your information, that occurred just a few years ago. We never stop learning my daughter.

All that we discuss here will make perfect sense to you, for you have that brilliant young mind that still "sees." As you grow older, hang on to what I am about to share with you. Seriously, this is "Secret Sauce." By that I mean, this is "life changing wisdom."

I have a deep question for you. Do you think a fish that has never been out of the water knows that it is wet? Take the anglerfish for example, that live in the deep ocean with long teeth and a light bulb on their head.

Some of those "fishies" like the anglerfish, live one-mile-deep in the ocean. Most of these fish have never been out of the water. They have no understanding of what it means to be wet, because they have never been dry. *I am kind of glad that these fish live in the deep. They are a bit scary!*

Ok Grasshopper, we are going to do a little experiment. If you feel uncomfortable, you can do the same experiment to me.

Ok, I want you to close your eyes. "Hello, close your eyes!" Keep them closed. Just sit there, listen, and of course breathe. Just relax. I will speak again in about five seconds.

Good. Now in a moment, I am going to ask you to take a deep breath through your nose. Make sure it is loud enough for me to hear. As you take the breath through your nose, count slowly to three in your head. I will count with you the first couple of times.

After you breathe in for three counts, I want you to just relax and let the air escape out of your mouth. Don't blow it out. Just relax, and let the air escape. Ok, ready?

Breathe in through the nose. One, two, three. Relax and let the air go out of your mouth. Do it again. Breathe in through the nose. One, two, three. Relax and let the air go out of your mouth. Again. Breathe in through the nose.

Relax and let the air go out of your mouth. Now keep that going while I continue reading to you.

Imagine that you are in the midst of nothingness. By that I mean pitch black, silent, and cold. There is no smell, nothing to touch, and nothing to taste. You don't feel anything about this nothingness. It is neither good nor bad. Nothing is in nothingness. "Nada." Got it?

The closest experience you have to this nothingness is when you are in a deep sleep, and you aren't dreaming.

Now, come back. Open your eyes slowly, look around and wiggle a little. Stretch your arms up high. Smile from ear to ear. Say your name.

Notice how different this moment is from the nothingness. You do notice the difference?

Right?

The words I am about to read to you come from a literary masterpiece entitled the *Tao Te Ching*. The *Tao Te Ching* was written more than 2,500 years ago, in China, by a man named Lao Tzu.

There are many legends about this guy, Lao Tzu. One legend says that he was born a wise, 60-something year-old man. If true, I wonder what his mom thought when she saw him for the first time. I can imagine him breathing his first breath and then saying "Hey mom, what's up?"

Wouldn't that be a shocker.

His name literally means "Old, Young."

To give you an idea just how important the *Tao Te Ching* is, the only book that has been translated into other languages more than the *Tao Te Ching* is the Bible. When you grow up, read the whole thing. Ok, let's check out some of the *Tao Te Ching*.

> When people see some things as beautiful,
> other things become ugly.
> When people see some things as good,
> other things become bad.
>
> Being and non-being create each other.
> Difficult and easy support each other.
> Long and short define each other.
> High and low depend on each other.
> Before and after follow each other.

Whoa Grasshopper, pretty cool thoughts, huh? Remember our question at the beginning about the fish? We could add to the *Tao Te Ching* this thought:

"When a fish is out of the water for the first time, only then does it desire to be wet."

That symbol at the top of this portion is of Chinese origin. It is known as yin yang which means "Light and Shadow."

Hmmm. This is about to get really interesting Grasshopper!

Have you ever really thought about shadows? You know, there is nothing there. Shadows aren't "real."

Stick with me, and what I am saying will make perfect sense.

Let's explore how to make a shadow. Let's explore how to make your shadow. First, we need a source of light such as the sun. Is that enough to see your shadow? Not yet.

Next, we need a surface upon which your shadow will appear, such as the ground. Still, no shadow.

The last thing we need to make your shadow, is you! We need you standing in the light of the sun. And there is your shadow cast upon the ground!

Here is where it gets interesting. The sun is a glowing sphere of hot gas, mostly hydrogen. It is very real; would you agree?

The ground of the earth where you stand is made of minerals and rotting dead stuff. The earth is very real; would you agree? And of course, you are real. But your shadow is not real. In fact, your shadow is made by taking away the light in the shape of you. In a sense, it is darkness in the shape of you.

It does not have weight. You cannot touch, taste or smell it. It cannot move independently. Your shadow is not something. Your shadow is something missing, and that something is light. And where there is no light, there is your shape.

Whoa!

Now, let's revisit some of those words from the *Tao Te Ching*.

"When people see some things as beautiful, other things become ugly." Ugly cannot exist without beauty. High cannot exist without low. Your shadow cannot exist without you. Interesting, isn't it? But what does this have to do with you? Everything.

You see Grasshopper, whatever you "know" you only can know because you also know about its opposite, its "shadow." Some refer to this as "Dualism" or "Taoism."

That yin yang symbol, which means light and shadow, expresses this beautifully. If you cut out the white part and cut out a little hole where the block dot is, the shadow it would make would be just like the dark part with a white dot on it. One part defines the other. The Tao Te Ching is saying the same thing, but with words.

Whoa!

Now here is where things get really, really interesting. Remember when we talked about your shadow not being real? Your shadow was created by removing light in the shape of you. So what, then, is darkness? The absence of light. What is silence? The absence of sound. What is cold? The absence of heat.

And, just like your shadow, only one item in each pair is "real." By real, I mean it has energy and exists within the physical realm. The other is the absence of the one that exists. To make a room dark, you switch the light off, which makes the light go away by stopping the flow of electricity. You do not turn the dark on, you remove the light.

This concept is also true for motion. You breathe in, you breathe out. You cannot do one without the other. The heart pumps blood away from the heart, and then it returns to the heart.

That is why you hear the thump-thump sound when you listen to a heartbeat.

The ocean waves rush on to the sand, only to return to the sea. You can't kick a soccer ball without first doing something to prepare to kick the ball. Each season is only possible because of the preceding season, and so it goes.

Love, I want to leave you with one last thought. These opposites that we have been talking about can never exist at the same time. You cannot have a room be both dark and light at the same time.

And zombies, the "living dead," are not real. *Right?*

You cannot be alive and dead at the same time. I just wanted to throw that in there in case the last chapter caused you to wonder about that.

Desire is light. Where there
is light, there can be no dark.

If you spend your energy on
what you do not want in life,
your path will be dark.
Stay focused on your desires,
and your path will be
illuminated.

DEAR DAUGHTER, YOU CANNOT WANT WHAT YOU DO NOT WANT

Dear Daughter,

I want to make a confession. For the first several weeks of your life, I was unable to see the brilliant genius you were.

"Gawrsh," I exclaimed in a goofy voice.

"She can't do nothing. She is just a blob. Ah-yuck! But she shore is beyootiful."

One of my goofiest moments by far.

Little did I know what was really going on. You were like a newly sprouted acorn, about to blast your way into a magnificent and mighty oak tree. You had been laying low, acting cool, looking like nothing was going on.

But on the inside, your roots had taken hold. You were readying yourself for something big.

Of course, sweet daughter, these are merely the observations of me, your father. No child has ever spoken within the first few weeks of their life. But, I would bet I have this right.

After those first few weeks, you became confident that your "survival needs" would be met by boobs, blankets, bedtimes, baths, binkies and other words that start with "b." Because of that confidence, you were free to start thinking about new things.

Your needs? Handled. It was time for you to pursue joy, fueled by your desires.

And then, it happened. Within a few short weeks of your birth, you did the most amazing thing. You did it without anyone teaching you. Your face glowed with the most beautiful, deep-from-within, smile. It was so lovely, and a little crooked and smirky. It was borderline mischievous, but in a completely innocent, fun way.

And your eyes, they twinkled like stars. When I saw those eyes, I was knocked to the floor.

I had it all wrong. You were not a babbling blob. I was!

I'm surprised I didn't wet my pants.

You however, were in a very different place and it was time for you to finally show it. "Game on Big Daddy. Life is good and about to get better. Hold on tight Daddy, because you and I are taking a ride."

The spirit you expressed on that day with your smile is the same spirit that drove you to crawl, walk, talk, ride your bike, and ask, "What's next?"

Believe it or not, all babies arrive with that spirit. All babies smile just like you did.

This is the same spirit that leads to inventions like iPhones and ensures that newer and improved versions are just around the corner. This is the same spirit that leads to new discoveries in science, such as finding a new planet or sun.

This is the same spirit that discovers new formulas in math.

I bet you love that.

This is why we will always have new music, art, plays, movies, architecture, and of course new styles for clothes.

Take a look at the clothes kids were wearing when I was a kid. Do you want to dress like that? It's okay. If I saw the clothes you kids were wearing when I was a kid, I wouldn't want to dress like that either. So, we're even!

The name of this spirit is desire. It is part of all that "lives," including you. All that the Creator created, creates. It is how we are made. This is why you were born demanding to be happy.

Though they haven't proved this yet, I just know it is part of our DNA. We are programmed to desire.

Our inner voice is always saying "What's next?"

Ok Grasshopper, get ready for this next part. If you desire a break for bathroom, burger or other words that start with b, now is the time. I want you to really "get" this next part. Life-changing stuff coming.

Remember when we were talking about light? Remember how you only know what light is because you know what it is like when there is no light? Absence-of-light is too much to say, so we named it "dark." And remember that beautiful fish that has no idea she is wet? Let her dry up a bit on the sand, and she will absolutely know wet.

Well, guess what Grasshopper? The same is true for each and every one of your desires. Whatever you desire, you desire because you can imagine how it feels to be without it.

You only want to eat when you feel hungry. After you have eaten and your tummy feels full, you don't feel the desire to eat again.

Right?

The same is true for that pair of shoes that you want so badly you "could die."

Your words, not mine.

When you walk out of the shoe store with those new shoes on your feet and a smile on your face, have you ever wanted to turn around and go back in that store for those same "life-saving" shoes? That desire is gone, at least for that moment. Isn't that cool?

Wanting something is an emotional experience, and it can feel really good. Recently you said "Oh my gosh, I want to go to New York during Christmas. I want to ice skate at The Rink at Rockefeller Center."

We haven't done that just yet, but when you spoke about that "dream," you were all giddy and excited. You were emotionally charged, just from thinking and speaking about that experience!

But, there is a flipside. Not having something that you want is also an emotional experience, and it can feel really bad. "I am never going to get to go to New York during Christmas. I am never going to go skating at The Rink at Rockefeller Center. I should just not want that anymore. It is never going to happen."

Now, which one of those two do you think is the better choice? Which one of those two do you think gives you the best chance to skate at The Rink at Rockefeller Center? Most importantly, which one of those two feels the best to you?

There is a trick to handling all that you want in life. Whatever you want to experience, want it! Think about that experience! Imagine it!

Just make sure that it is what you want, and not what someone else has convinced you to want. On the other hand, when you want something, but all you can think about is the fact that you don't have it, stop thinking about it. Chill. Do something else. And, when you are in a good peaceful place, like right before you fall asleep, imagine how wonderful it is going to be when you have it. *Milk those feelings like you would a Jersey Cow.*

Now Grasshopper, I want you to think of what you want as light. Now, think of not having what you want as its shadow. What you want is buzzing with energy! What you want, but hurt because you don't have it, is nothingness. It just so happens, that the nothingness is formed in the shape of what you want.

This is just like your shadow that is formed in the shape of you. You are real. Your shadow is not.

What you want is real. Feeling lack, is not. One will move you forward, and the other will trap you.

I know, I know. "But dad, not having those cool shoes that everyone else has does not feel like nothing. It stings!" Yes, it does, but for how long and how much depends on you. Let's take this to a new level.

Let's think about anyone that you believe is great at what they do. By great, I mean so great, that they will be remembered long after they have left this world.

I am talking about "game changers!" These people might be artists, inventors, musicians, actors, doctors, inventors, presidents; they might be anything. When any of these game changing people talk about their beliefs, they all say the same thing!

"Champions aren't made in gyms. Champions are made from something deep inside them. A desire, a dream, a vision."

"The first step before anybody else in the world believes it is you have to believe it."

Muhammad Ali (1942–2016)
Considered The Greatest Boxer of All Time

"Be thankful for what you have. . . you'll end up having more. If you concentrate on what you don't have. . . you will never, ever have enough."

Oprah Winfrey (1954–)
Talk Show Host, Producer, Philanthropist, Actress

"Nothing can stop a man with the right mental attitude from achieving his goal."

Will Smith (1968–)
American Author, Actor, Singer, Producer

"I actually finally let the Light in and then I was able to create all these songs that were inspired by letting the Light in...."

Katy Perry (1984–)
Singer, Songwriter

✦ ✦ ✦

"I am not what happened to me. I am what I choose to become."

Thomas Jefferson (1743–1826)
American Founding Father (1776)

✦ ✦ ✦

"When one door of happiness closes, another opens; but often we look so long at the closed door that we do not see the one which has been opened for us."

Helen Keller (1880–1968)
Educator, Journalist, she was Blind and Deaf

✦ ✦ ✦

"The limits are only what you can imagine."

Abraham Lincoln (1809–1865)
President, The Emancipation of Slaves

✦ ✦ ✦

"A new journey to be started.
A new promise to be fulfilled.
A new page to be written.
Go forth unto this waiting world with pen in hand, all
you young scribes,
the open book awaits.
Be creative.
Be adventurous.
Be original.
And above all else, be young.
For youth is your greatest weapon, your greatest tool.
Use it wisely."

Wonder Woman (1941–)
The Most Popular Female Comic-Book Superhero

"Your will turns thought in to reality. To master the
ring, you must learn to focus your will and create what
you see in your mind."

The Green Lantern (1940–)
Male Superhero

"Don't lose faith in what you are trying to do, even though you will get pummeled emotionally left and right. There are a lot of NOs to any YES. And that's OK."

Jennifer Lee (1971–)
Wrote the Screenplay for "Frozen" (2013)

✦✦✦

"I don't dream at night; I dream all day. I dream for a living."

Steven Spielberg (1946–)
Screenwriter, Director, Producer

✦✦✦

"All that we are is a result of what we have thought."

Buddha (Forever)
Awakened One

✦✦✦

"Therefore, I tell you, whatever you ask for in prayer, believe that you have received it, and it will be yours."

Jesus Christ (Forever)
Son of God, Messiah

✦✦✦

"O... M... G!!!" Get it? Contained within those quotes is the formula to happiness. Here are every one of those quotes, restated in "dad speak."

1) Decide what you want in life. Dream about what you want in life. Envision what you want in life, and you will have it.

My daughter, you will be victorious.

2) The only thing that matters is that you believe in you.

3) Be thankful every single day, no matter what that day is like. A thankful heart gets more. And when more comes, be thankful again. The more you are thankful, the more you will have; more joy, more happiness, more of everything.

4) Get your thoughts right, and nothing can stand in your way.

5) Let go of thoughts that create hatred. Let go of judging anyone, including yourself. Let go of placing conditions on your happiness. Instead, be full of hope in all situations. Be patient with others, for they are on their own path. Be kind. Be uplifting. Be humble. Do this, and the power of the Creator will flow through you like a river of light, and you will channel that creativity in amazing ways.

6) You were given the greatest and most loving gift imaginable. You were given the gift to choose your life. Receive that gift and your life will happen for you and because of you.

7) Nothing lasts forever. When things change, see that change as a giftwrapped present, and then open it.

8) The only limitations that you have in life are the ones you create. Dare to dream big!

9) You are the author of your own story. Hold on to that. Stay in tune with those wonderful traits that you possessed when you were born. Be adventurous, youthful, playful, creative, and true to only you and what you want. There is only one you.

10) All that is and has ever happened, first started with a thought. Any thought might become your reality. Choose your thoughts with this knowledge.

11) You are going to encounter gobs of naysayers throughout your life. Take it as a compliment, and don't spend one drop of sweat trying to change their minds. Instead, use that negativity to believe in yourself even more.

12) Your imagination is one of the most pleasurable and powerful tools that you possess. No matter how much you use it, you will never run out of imagination.

And it is free!

Use it like crazy. Use it all the time. Imagine happiness. Imagine fun. Imagine hope. Imagine creativity. Seriously! It is like a wishing well.

13) Own your life, good and bad. Take responsibility for all that has happened. The moment that you can do this, it will change the way you choose to think for the rest of your days. Trust me my daughter, you will focus on the good thoughts.

14) Don't get all caught up in difficult times. Instead, imagine what you want from your life and feel the emotional joy right then. The future that is coming to you, is the one that you can imagine, believe, and feel now.

My darling daughter, it doesn't matter if you are: poor or rich, black, white, red, brown or yellow, or all-girl or tomboy. There are no disadvantages, unless you choose to create one.

It doesn't matter if you read books with your eyes or with your fingers by touching dots. It doesn't matter if you talk with spoken words or you use sign language. It doesn't matter if you move around on legs or roll around on wheels. There are no disadvantages, unless you choose to create one.

Got it Grasshopper? Do ya?

Your life and how it goes is a choice, your choice. How awesome is that? You get to choose!

Along your journey through life, you are going to occasionally feel hurt. I get it.

Hurting sucks raw eggs, your daddy really does understands.

Sometimes the hurt feels really, really bad. The question is, "How long do you keep thinking about the hurt?"

Trust me. It takes the same amount of energy to think a "yucky thought" as it does to think a good thought. But, only one of those will turn out wonderfully. And, since a yucky thought brings more yucky thoughts, you will feel really yucky. You will use more energy over time.

And, please stay away from movies, music, books, people, zombies and anything else that expresses a message of fear or hopelessness. If you eat trash, you are going to get sick. If you feed your mind trash, your mind is going to get sick.

When you do encounter an experience that stings you emotionally, distract yourself. Not forever, just for a little while until the sting doesn't sting so much.

Remember that there are those emotional decomposers that are breaking that experience down. Give yourself a little time! Let the decomposers do their work. Kittens on the internet, funny movies, or watching kids at play are some of my favorite distractions.

Before you know it, you will be able think about that hurtful experience rationally, and get your thoughts back on track. But when you first feel the sting, you need to give yourself a little break.

And for goodness sake, never ever tell a hopeless story! Never post a pathetic tale on the internet!

You will be tempted to tell the whole world about your pain, during some of those stinging moments. But, no matter what, "Do not do it!" Oh, and, "Do not do it." And, whatever you do, "Do not do that."

Have I made my point?

Just as a happy girl attracts others that are happy, the same is true for the miserable. Do you really want to think of yourself or have others think of you as a hopeless miserable person?

Grasshopper, I have a challenge for you, and I think you will find this fun and funny. You will be shocked at what this challenge reveals to you.

For one week, I want you to only express what you want... not what you do not want. How? You must avoid using the words "do not want" or "don't want."

If I ask you what you want to eat for lunch, say what you want. Do not say "Well, I don't want [fill in the blank]."

If we have 4 pieces of pizza and 5 people, see how we can divide that pizza up for everyone. See abundance instead of lack. Do not say, "I don't think we can make it work. That is not enough."

Have fun with this Love. You will be amazed how often we express what we want in the form of what we do not want. You can't do that. You can't want what you do not want.

See? See?

Love,

Dad

KEY 4

Overcoming Obstacles Through Invention

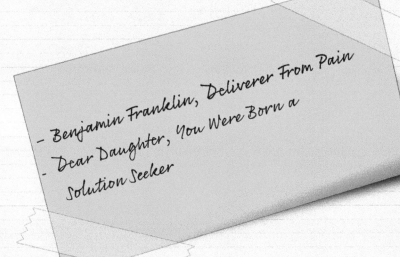

— Benjamin Franklin, Deliverer From Pain

— Dear Daughter, You Were Born a Solution Seeker

Everyone knows about Benjamin Franklin's kite flying experiment in a thunderstorm. But there is so much more that this amazing man accomplished.

When Benjamin encountered an obstacle of any kind, he set his thoughts on finding a solution.

BENJAMIN FRANKLIN, DELIVERER FROM PAIN

In the last chapter, we learned how "opposites" define all that we know, including our desires. I thought this would be the perfect time to talk about Benjamin Franklin.

He used the "pains and hardships" that were common during his lifetime, to inspire his solutions and inventions. Instead of focusing on what was not wanted, Benjamin focused on what he wanted.

Get it?

I know, I know what you are thinking. Benjamin Franklin is that potbellied, nerdy guy with a funny hairdo. "I can't argue with you there."

And you probably think that he invented electricity. He didn't invent electricity, but he did discover many of its properties.

He is the guy that tied a metal key to a kite and flew it in a storm.

"True dat."

A one-hundred-dollar bill is nicknamed a "Benjie" because his face is on it.

Personally, I think he might be a relative of Mona Lisa. I mean, just look at how similarly they smile.

And that is probably everything you know about him. And no, Benjamin was never President of the United States.

I want to tell you about this amazing person and his many achievements. Let's start at the beginning of his life.

Bennie Boy was born in 1706 in Boston, Massachusetts. His dad made soap and candles for a living. His dad, get ready for this one, had 17 children between two wives. "Let that soak in for a moment." Can you imagine having 16 brothers and sisters?

Benjamin's father's first wife died after giving birth to her seventh child. Since there were 17 children born to Benjamin's father, that would mean his second wife had how many children? "I hope you said 10."

Benjamin was his father's fifteenth child. His mother was the second wife of his father. He was her eighth child.

Man, Benjamin's birth should be one of those math story problems.

Do you think Benjamin had a lot of quality time with his parents? *I mean, there are three of you and you all feel like there is not enough of me to go around. Imagine if there were 17 of you.*

Do you think his family had a lot of money? Making soap and candles was no way to get rich in those days, even with one kid. "Imagine what it was like with seventeen."

Benjamin started grammar school at age 8, but within a year, finances were getting tight for dear old dad. *Grammar school is kind of like your elementary school. You were in the third grade when you were 8 years old.*

Around the time that Benjamin was 9 years old, he was pulled from grammar school, and moved to a less expensive school that only taught writing and arithmetic. No history, science, music, or art. Just reading, writing and math.

By the time Benjamin turned 10, dear old dad's finances changed from tight to "snuggie" tight.

Sometimes older brothers will pull a younger brother's underwear out of the back of his pants, and stretch the waistband all the way up to his neck, leaving the younger brother with no wiggle room. This is called a "snuggie."

I am not saying that your uncles did this to me, and I am not saying that they did not do this. I'm just sayin'. But the description sure is useful to describe the financial situation of Ben's father. No wiggle room, out of choices!

Ben's father had no wiggle room. He was going broke fast. Ben's father made 10-year-old Benjamin drop out of school so he could work for the good of the family. This very smart, well spoken, educated man was in school for only a few years.

And no, you can't drop out of school so just let that go.

The rest of Ben's learning, he achieved on his own through reading, and through his interactions with others. In other words, Benjamin was homeschooled and was both the student and the teacher.

The dude loved to read by the way. During his time, there were no radios, TVs, iPods or movie theaters. Benjamin's reading was a form of entertainment.

Let me share with you some of Benjamin Franklin's achievements. The same Ben that dropped out of school around what you know of as the fifth grade. Many of these achievements will be familiar to you.

From a very young age, Ben was quite the swimmer. We humans are not engineered for fast swimming. We have fingers instead of webbed hands. We have feet with toes instead of flippers. We are aquatically challenged; the slow pokes of the water.

Losing swim races to dolphins probably frustrated little Ben, and this frustration led to his very first invention. At the wee age of 11, he invented swimming fins. His version of swimming fins was worn on the hands, but it didn't take long for others to take his idea and move the fins to the feet. That year was 1717.

Benjamin loved reading. What you might not know however, is that books were not easy things to get into one's hands during his early years. There were no Barnes and Nobles or libraries.

I have a feeling that Benjamin read books faster than he could buy them. So, Benjamin set up the first library in America. This library had members, and everyone had to pitch in to buy books.

See?

"More people, more money, more books for everyone involved." That year was 1731.

There were lots of fires during Ben's lifetime. These fires were usually caused by lightning, fireplaces, candles, and lanterns. When Benjamin was living in Philadelphia, he set up that city's first volunteer fire department called the Union Fire Company.

The Union Fire Company had several firemen that became very famous about 40 years later. You might have heard of some of them: George Washington, Thomas Jefferson, our friend Benjamin Franklin, Samuel Adams, John Hancock, Paul Revere, Alexander Hamilton, John Jay, John Barry, Aaron Burr, Benedict Arnold (boo hiss), James Buchanan and Millard Fillmore. That year was 1736.

There were no heaters during Benjamin's lifetime. The winters in the colonies were long and very cold. They had fireplaces, but they did not work very well. They required a tremendous amount of wood which meant someone had to chop down a lot of trees.

Fireplaces caused many fires. The fireplaces did not work very well. Most of the heat went straight up the chimney. Sometimes a draft of wind would blow down the chimney and fill the home with smoke. What did Benjamin do?

Benjamin invented the Franklin Stove. This stove was made of cast iron, and was created with some groovy engineering.

Benjamin's design extracted more heat from the fire than the typical fireplace, and it used fewer logs. This stove also enclosed the burning logs, which made them safer than an open fireplace. Believe it or not, the Franklin Stove is still used around the world today. That year was 1742.

Philadelphia, where Benjamin lived, was a fast growing city with lots of people living there. The city's infrastructure couldn't quite keep up. The people were peeing, pooping and making garbage faster than the city could handle. The population of the poor and mentally ill people also grew.

Many ships sailed between Philadelphia and Europe. There were lots of travelers with diseases not common in America. That meant that the immune system of the those living in America did not have a lot of experience fighting off those diseases from overseas. Lots of people got sick.

All of this combined, created the perfect storm for sickness and disease. "What did Benjamin do?" Benjamin co-founded the first hospital in America, the Pennsylvania Hospital. That year was 1751.

Next comes the moment you have been waiting for, Benjamin's kite flying experiment in a storm. He did this to prove his theory that lightning was electricity. I imagine almost everyone else who might have touched lightning directly didn't live to tell about it. Franklin used a metal key, and he still got quite a shock.

"At least he lived to tell the truth!"

Lightning was definitely electricity. That year was 1752.

After Benjamin proved his theory that lightning was electricity, he created the lightning rod. The lightning rod was basically a sharp pointed metal pole placed on top of a building or house. One end of a long wire was attached to the pole, and the other end was buried in the ground.

You see, lightning is attracted to tall objects in the area where it is about to strike. Before Benjamin created the lightning rod, the tallest objects were usually the roofs of homes or a church steeple. In those days, churches and homes were built with wood, and wood burns you know... lots of fires in those days.

You get it.

Electricity likes metal more than wood. It moves better through metal. You might have studied about conduction. Metal is a good conductor of electricity. And thanks to Benjamin, we know that lightning is electricity. You see where this is going.

Right?

Benjamin's lightning rods were placed on the tops of churches and houses. Since the lightning rod had some length, it extended higher than the church or house. And since the lightning rod was made of metal, "Go ahead, take a guess."

Hmm, tall object, made of metal. Lightning is attracted to tall objects, and it is attracted to metal.

Instead of striking the wooden church or home, the lightning would strike the lightning rod. The lightning would travel through the rod, all the way down the wire, and end harmlessly in the ground. As a result, the church or home was safe. These are still used today! "How strikingly slick is that?" That year was 1752.

Before going on to yet another of Benjamin's achievements, let's pause to talk about lightning safety. Where we live, there is a lot of lightning.

1) If you are outside when lightning is striking nearby, get inside a substantial structure such as a building if you can. If the only choice you have is a car, get in it.

2) Whether you are in a car, house, or some structure like a building, stay away from metal. If you are in a car, stay away from seatbelt buckles, metallic knobs and handles, and the pedals. If you are in a home or structure, avoid the telephone land line, sinks and showers. Also, avoid the ovens, fridges, and other stuff that has metal.

3) If you are in the middle of nowhere when the lightning strikes are coming, look for a low ditch and crouch down as low as you can, and stay down!

4) Do not get under a tree. Trees are tall.

5) Umbrellas are not a good idea when lightning is striking. The tip of an umbrella is usually made of metal. Lightning likes metal. Remember?

6) Do not get in small structures like port-a-potties. I mean, why would you anyway? The smell is a warning to stay away!

7) Your hair standing on end during a storm is a sign that lightning is about to strike close to you.

8) Wherever you find safety, remain there until at least 30 minutes has passed since the last lightning strike.

This dad thing never ends. So much to teach, so much to share. I love it!

Ok, let's get back to the history lesson, and talk about another one of Benjamin's inventions. Benjamin's next achievement was created only for pleasure. It did not solve a problem. Sometimes, we get inspired to do something because it feels good or is just plain cool. We create for the enjoyment.

Benjamin invented a musical instrument called an armonica, which is not anything like a harmonica. Touching spinning crystal bowls with a wet finger is how one played the armonica.

Believe it or not, Mozart and Beethoven both composed music for the armonica. This was Ben's favorite invention by the way! That year was 1762.

Benjamin invented what might very well be the first Transformer in Colonial America. Look out Optimus Prime, here comes Library Chair. *Wow, Library Chair is a pretty wimpy sounding Transformer.*

Ben had a lot of books. So many in fact, that he had to keep some on shelves out of his reach. When Benjamin was reading, he would sit in a chair. When Benjamin needed to access a book that was slightly out of his reach, he would get out of the chair and use his stepladder.

It seems a bit inconvenient to have to get a stepladder out, use it and put it back, every time you want to read a book that is out of reach. Plus, stepladders are a bit bulky. Benjamin invented a chair with a reversible seat that could also serve as a small stepladder, "a two in one thingamajig." Believe it or not, you can still buy one of these today on Amazon. That year was around 1768.

Hang in there Love, just two more to go in this history lesson. Believe it or not, I left out many things that Benjamin did.

Benjamin needed glasses to read and to see. This meant that he had to carry around two pairs of glasses. If he was reading, he put on his reading glasses. If he was looking down the street, he put on his regular glasses.

All day long he was switching glasses.

"What a pain!"

Benjamin asked his optometrist to saw the lenses of both glasses in half. He connected the bottom part of the reading glasses to the top part of the seeing glasses, and on that day bifocals were born. That year was 1784.

You might notice a bit of a gap between those last two, 1762 and 1784. Benjamin was preoccupied with a little o' thing, helping with the birth of The United States of America. He played a very active role in that. Without his contributions, we might not have made it.

This next one is going to crack you up. You know those funny toys that have a handle that you squeeze, and it makes a hand on the end of a rod, close and open? You know the ones. You can win them at the fair, or at those youth-gambling training-places, where you spin wheels and roll balls for tickets that you exchange at great expense for really cheap prizes.

Ben invented those "hands-on-a-stick" around the age of 76. He called it the Long Arm. He invented the Long Arm so he could reach the books stored high in the shelves of the library. That was in the year 1786.

The list goes on and on. This guy did not view the difficult parts of life as difficult. Instead, he chose to innovate. For Benjamin, problems and difficulty were sources of inspiration.

"Pretty cool, huh?"

As you continue to grow up, you might think history sucks.

"It doesn't."

Some of the teachers that teach history might suck, but the stories they are teaching do not. Your story does not suck, and it is the story of history for some young mind of a future generation.

My story, before you were born, is history for you.

"Look at it that way, and dig in to those amazing stories."

There were little ones, just like you living way back when. They are all now part of your amazing story, including Benjamin Franklin.

Every challenge that you face is like
a door that only you can unlock.
Behind that door is a room with
something wonderful in it.
And on the other side of that room
is another door.

The more doors you unlock,
the more wonderful life becomes.

DEAR DAUGHTER, YOU WERE BORN A SOLUTION SEEKER

Dear Daughter,

When you were a baby, I watched you struggle to roll over and I thought how hard of a task this was for you. Yet, I knew you could do it and indeed you did; splendidly I might add. At least once you rolled off the bed and plopped on the floor, but you continued to roll over without fear of a fall.

In case you are wondering, you cried, but only for a moment. Though you were not yet using words, I could feel the language of your heart speak loudly, "More, more, more!"

And then you worked on a more advanced task, crawling. Again, I thought how hard this must be for you, even more difficult than rolling over. But you knew you could do it, and indeed you did.

You crawled so much that one of your knees became raw. Yet, you still wouldn't stop. And you, a natural born genius, found a way to compensate for your raw knee. What did you do? You started dragging your good knee while you kept your other knee off the ground.

You reminded me of a baby gorilla scooching through a forest.

Thinking about that memory still makes my chuckle.

No fear or pain could keep you from crawling. And your heart shouted with joy, "More, more, more!"

And then came the walking. Your bumps and bruises were far greater in number and severity than what you experienced when rolling or crawling. At least five times, a dog much larger than you knocked you flat on your back. I thought how hard this must be for you, but you knew you could do it.

None of the bumps and bruises mattered to you. You always got back up. Joy, your purpose for being here, was far too powerful for bumps and bruises to stand in your way. And you continued expressing from your heart, "More, more, more!"

As you grow older, life will continue to bring you, "More, more, more!" Rolling over, crawling, walking running, skipping? Been there, done that. Soon it will be driving, relationships, higher education, sports, inventing, learning, traveling, maybe raising a family, and more. Truth be told, there are endless possibilities for you to experience in life.

And just as it was with rolling, crawling, and walking, these other experiences will also come with some bumps and bruises. The trick is to maintain that same, "More, more, more!" spirit that you showed during your early years.

As you grow older, you will notice that the "can do anything" attitude becomes a "can't do" attitude for many people. You will also notice that those people can't do very much.

Hmm.

On the flipside, you will notice that a minority of people keep right on cruising through the "bumps and bruises." You will also notice that these people are superstars within their chosen domain. By that, I mean their passions, upon which they have directed their life.

It does not matter if their passion is sewing, parenting or playing baseball. These people are giants. These people continue to shout, "More, more, more!" These people believe in themselves.

Can you imagine a future President of the United States saying, "Gosh, I just don't know if I can lead this country. It sure is tough, and sometimes I get my feelings hurt."

Presidents might not always make decisions with which you agree. But whatever decisions they make, they do so with confidence.

Benjamin Franklin never lost that "can do anything" attitude. From his early childhood until he was the long-haired, bald-on-top, pot-bellied nerdy guy that you know him as, he never stopped finding ways around obstacles.

And just to let you know, I left out a bunch of his achievements, for fear of putting you to sleep with a history lesson.

You and I will never know Benjamin Franklin personally. He is long dead.

Right?

But we can know about his passions. How? By observing his achievements.

Did he have a passion for the well-being of others? Absolutely. Hospitals and fire stations serve people, not any one person.

Did the risk of a fire influence Benjamin? Big time. Not only did he try to put them out with the help of his fellow firemen, but he invented the lightning rod to prevent them. Go ahead and throw his stove in there as well.

Was he practical?

That is probably a new word to you. It means to care about how we use common things or do common tasks.

Bifocals and his transforming chair-ladder would say yes. Was he fun? Armonically fun! Swimming fin fun!

My little Einstein, Benjamin has nothing over you. You are born a genius too. No, you might not care about fires, electricity, reading, or the practical things of life. But, there is only one person on the planet like you. That makes you uniquely brilliant. Stay true to your passions.

Let me say that once more. Stay true to your passions, not the passions others think you should have.

Do this, and you will see solutions when presented with obstacles. Every day will be filled with moments of inspiration. It doesn't matter if your solution is "the next greatest invention," or a way to make studying for a history fun and efficient.

Focus on your attitude, and the solutions you produce will be exactly right. It really is nothing more than a habit. You were born that way.

Remember?

And for Pete's sake, do not listen to naysayers.

When my dad, your granddad, needed to remember to take something with him the next morning to work, he would tie that something to his car keys. As far as I know, he never forgot his morning cargo except maybe one time, which inspired the solution. He also did some pretty slick solution solving for NASA. It is the same solution-mind at work, whether seemingly "big" or "small."

Love,

Dad

KEY 5

Time Traveling to the Future

- The Time Machine
- Dear Daughter, Travel to the Future Wisely

This is one of the first of many covers that adorned this H.G. Wells' science fiction classic, written in 1895.

Science fiction writers are masters of the imagination. We can learn a lot from these visionaries about the creating of futuristic worlds.

THE TIME MACHINE

In the last chapter, we talked about the amazing Benjamin Franklin and his many achievements and inventions. This seems like a very good time to talk to you about an invention that has not been invented yet. Someday it will be a reality.

I am talking about a time machine. Since time machines haven't been invented yet, we are going to explore a science fiction novella, *The Time Machine*, written in 1895 by H.G. Wells, the creator of science fiction.

Now before you turn your nose up, remember that your dad enjoys princesses and ponies just as much as you, so give science fiction a chance.

Science fiction is cool. You might think science fiction is just some fantasy stuff that usually takes place in the future or involves time travel or portals. Indeed, that assumption is true. That makes sense when you think about it.

Some sci-fi stories mirror those fairy tales of old. You know, the "good versus evil" fairy tales, and in the end good always wins. They are loaded with a variety of colorful characters such as magical beasts, monsters, mythical beings, fairies, elves, mystics, wizards and witches, princesses and princes, villains, heroes, prophets, and more. The "Star Wars" saga is a perfect example of this type of sci-fi.

Other sci-fi stories present those "what if" scenarios that have not yet happened. Obviously, if a tale is about something that has not yet happened, the best setting is in the future. If it does not take place in the future, then a parallel world or universe, or some location where extraterrestrials hang out is a good choice.

Whatever the setting, it is one that we have not experienced. This is a big advantage for sci-fi authors. Using their imagination, the writers get to make up "unseen" worlds as they tell their story.

In these "what if" sci-fi stories, the writers are usually trying to make a point about some part of present life by telling us what the future will be like if we don't change our ways. Sometimes, these stories are ironic and funny, and the endings are usually a bit scary.

The "what if" sci-fi writers seem to be giving us a warning.

"If we don't change, this could happen."

Using this technique, sci-fi writers can cause us to think about situations from a different perspective. *The Time Machine* by H.G. Wells is one of these "what if" stories.

Before we look more closely at *The Time Machine* story, I need to tell you why I said that someday there will be real time machines. Believe it or not, one of the greatest geniuses that ever lived proved that it was possible to travel into the future, sort of.

Actually, what he proved was something called time dilation. He proved that if a person could travel almost at the speed of light, time slows down.

For example, pretend that I have a super-fast rocket that can travel almost as fast as light. On my rocket, I have enough food for 3 meals a day for a thousand days. I also have a special little watch that counts how many days I have been traveling in my rocket.

I board the rocket, and I wave to you out the window. The count-down commences: ten, nine, eight, seven, six, five, four, three, two, one, blastoff!

In an instant, I am gone. I make this humongous loop in space, and after 1,000 days, I come back to earth landing exactly where I left. I am so excited to see you! I have been looking at my special watch every day. Finally, it reached 1,000 days. *By the way, 1,000 days away from you is way too long.*

As soon as my rocket ship door opens, I jump out and shout your name as loudly as I can. But instead of seeing you as I remember you 1,000 days ago, I see an old lady standing there saying in a warbled soft voice, "Daddy, I missed you!"

That old lady is you. I am 1,000 days older, and you are 30 or 40 years older. Time slowed down for me, but time kept trucking along at the usual speed for you.

"Weird, huh?"

The genius that proved this to be true was Albert Einstein, with his famous equation $E = mc^2$.

In H.G. Wells' *The Time Machine*, the main character referred to as The Time Traveler, travels in a time machine to the future year of 802,701. When The Time Traveler arrives in that year, he meets two different types of living creatures.

The first creature he meets is called the Eloi (pronounced Ee-loy). The Eloi are beautiful and without blemish. They are frail, small, child-sized adults. The Eloi eat only fruits, and they do absolutely nothing except play in very simple ways.

They all live together in a big room, and they are afraid of the dark. The Eloi aren't curious like you are. Heck, they hardly have an imagination.

The Eloi don't learn, problem-solve, or create. Every need they have is provided for them, so it really doesn't matter I suppose.

Have you ever heard the phrase, "Use it or lose it"? Those Eloi lost "it." They lost their zest for living. They probably consider the act of lifting a banana to their mouths a form of exercise. They are big-time wimps. Scary.

The other creatures The Time Traveler encounters are also scary, but in a completely different way. These other creatures are called Morlocks. They are kind of like hairy, big-eyed cavemen with long ugly pointed teeth.

"Icky icky."

The Morlocks only come out at night. During the day they stay in their caves underground. Their caves are completely dark, but the Morlocks don't mind. They can see in the dark with their big eyes. Here is the gross part. The Morlocks eat the Eloi.

Since the Eloi eat fruits, the Morlocks get their meat and fruits when they eat the Eloi.

"Pretty smart huh?"

This of course is why the Eloi are afraid of the dark. But the Eloi can't seem to figure out how to avoid being some Morlock's midnight snack. Now if all of this wasn't weird enough, this story gets even weirder.

Recall that those Eloi are a bunch of lazy bone wimps that have every need provided for them.

"Who do you think provides for their needs?"

"Who makes sure they have plenty to eat?"

"Who makes sure their things are clean and that they are comfortable?"

"Who makes sure their plumbing and electricity work?"

The Morlocks do! Yes, the ones that eat them also take care of their every need.

I know this sounds bizarre, but think about it like a herd of cattle. We raise cattle and take very good care of them. We make sure they have plenty to eat, and we do everything we can to keep them from getting sick. We help them and we help them and we help them, and then we eat them in the form of steaks, hamburgers, and more.

Yes, Morlocks and Eloi are kind of like us and cattle. Morlocks are the cattle ranchers and the Eloi are the cattle.

I know this story sounds a bit like a nightmare of a future. Nightmare futures are this type of science fiction's specialty. Endings that include the words "happily ever after," not so much.

Even though the writers of this style of science fiction paint these bleak futures, their intent is not to make you believe in those futures. Their intent is to inspire you to think in a new way, about something that is currently going on.

I have seen and read a boatload of science fiction stories, and not once did I think, "Kill me now! The future is without hope." I did however, think about the writer's topic from a different perspective. Let's look more closely at the Morlocks and Eloi, and you will see what I mean.

The Morlock and Eloi seem like they are two completely different species, and indeed they are. However, these two species were at one time the same as you and me, human beings. But in this story, and with more than 800,000 years to work with, H.G. Wells was able to make humans physically change over time. They evolved from one species into two, as in evolution.

Now you must be wondering how people like us could change into two new species like the Morlocks and Eloi. You are curious, right my lovely turtle? I mean, you are nothing like those Eloi.

You see, as long as there have been people, there have been some that do very well and some that do not. We can call them the Haves and the Have-Nots. That is just how things are and there is not necessarily anything wrong with that reality. Some people choose to be happy, while others choose to not be happy.

What is messed up, however, is when those who are doing well take advantage of those who are not. They try to prevent them from pursuing their own happiness and dreams.

It does not matter if a person is big or little, fast or slow, green or blue, speaks Martian or Jupiterian, knows a lot or a little, has no legs or three. We all have access to the same Power that I am sharing with you in this book. We all can choose thoughts of light or thoughts of dark. You will experience a life like you think.

But it is not right to take away another person's right to choose what they want out of their life. For one group of people to try and deny others the right to access the Power is yucky, really yucky. It is also yucky for one group of people to try and deny others the right to choose a powerless life. People have the right to choose their life, even if that choice is to be miserable.

Should we encourage others? Absolutely! Force others? Absolutely not! We were all born free, and no one has the right to take that freedom away from another!

History is full of examples where one group of people tried to exert their power over others and take their freedoms away. In every case, the group that oppressed others either changed or they ceased to exist. Yes, there are some oppressive people today that are still in power, but their time is coming. It is only a matter of time.

In *The Time Machine* however, the writer shows us a future when the oppressive people never lost their power. In *The Time Machine* the Eloi were the Haves after they evolved 800,000 plus years, and the Morlocks were the Have-Nots.

Listen my sweet little "Rip Van Twinkle" toes," 800,000 years is a looooooong time. If the Haves and the Have-Nots shared one significant change every hundred years, that would be 8,000 changes to life as we know it.

"Heck, let me see if I can even think of 10."

Let's pretend that we have two groups of people. Group A will be the "Haves" and Group B will be the Have-Nots.

For one hundred years, Group B washes all of the dishes for both groups. Within that one hundred years, the older people die and the new people are born. At the end of the one hundred years, no one in Group A even knows what washing dishes is like, because they never had to wash dishes.

For the next one hundred years, Group B kept washing dishes for Group A. They also started washing all of Group A's clothes. Same as before, old people die and new people are born. Now after two hundred years, no one from Group A knows how to wash dishes or clothes.

The next one hundred years, Group B did all the grocery shopping for Group A. They also kept washing their dishes and clothes. Same as before. The old die, new are born. Three hundred years have passed, and no one from Group A can wash dishes and clothes, or go to the store.

The next one hundred years, Group B did all the driving for Group A. They also kept doing all the other stuff for four hundred years.

Next one hundred years, Group B started doing homework, paying bills, making repairs, and other day-to-day tasks. Five hundred years passed by.

Next one hundred years, Group B went to work in place of Group A. Group B still gave Group A their paychecks, even though Group A no longer had a need for money. Six hundred years passed by.

Next one hundred years, Group B carried out the trash. Seven hundred years passed. Next one hundred years, Group B did all the cooking. Eight hundred years passed by. Next one hundred years, Group B fixed anything that was broken. Nine hundred years passed. Next one hundred years, Group B raised Group A's children.

Let that soak in for a minute. We just went through 1,000 years of changes. At the end of those 1,000 years, Group A is clueless about the most basic of skills.

1) They don't know how to wash dishes or clothes.

2) They don't know how to shop at a grocery store, and they don't know how to cook.

3) They don't know how to drive.

4) They don't know how to pay their bills or do homework.

5) They no longer go to work.

6) They don't take out the trash.

7) They don't know how to fix things in need of repair.

8) They don't even raise their own children.

The Time Machine takes place more than 800,000 years in the future. We just went through some pretty substantial changes in 1,000 years. I would have to keep doing that 800 more times to get to 800,000 years.

Now, here is something very interesting for you to ponder. After the 1,000 years of changes I provided above, which group is the most skillful? Which group most likely created better ways to wash clothes and dishes? Which group was more creative in every way? Which group created new inventions? Which group experienced life the most? Which group was more advanced? Group B.

Sweetheart, that is deep.

This is exactly what *The Time Machine* by H.G. Wells expresses. The Haves will work very little yet will have so much. As a result, they will regress. The Have-Nots must work very hard, yet they will have so little. Thus, they will advance.

But to really drive things home, H.G. Wells used the evolution of the human species. In *The Time Machine* the human species split into two different species.

It is worth mentioning that in 1859, Charles Darwin presented his ideas on evolution to the world in his work *The Origin of the Species*. This book sent a shockwave around the world that is still being felt today.

H.G. Wells wrote *The Time Machine* almost 45 years later, in 1895. Obviously, he incorporated evolution in this novella.

The Haves of the far-off future in *The Time Machine* physically changed. They became tiny little weaklings with very little muscle. If you don't use your body and muscles, your body no longer develops in those areas.

And since the Haves in the future stopped using their brains, they lost the ability to perform intellectually at a high level. They became vegetables. They became the Eloi.

What about the Have-Nots of the same, far off future? They changed physically too. Since they did everything for the Haves, their muscles and bones were very well developed. They were strong, tall, and physically superior.

Since the Have-Nots were doing all the thinking and problem-solving for the Eloi, they also became superior intellectually. And they were well organized as a group.

The Have-Nots also developed some physical characteristics, due to living in their underground cave dwellings. They became very hairy, and they developed the ability to see in the dark.

Their teeth were pointy and could tear raw flesh apart. These came in handy when eating filet Eloi, ultra-rare. According to H.G. Wells, the Have-Nots became the Morlocks.

Morlocks and the Eloi were two different species that evolved from one, us.

So why did H.G. Wells write *The Time Machine*? What was he trying to tell us? What is the real story behind the story *The Time Machine*?

H.G. Wells was born dirt-poor in England in 1866, at a time when the Industrial Revolution was in full force. If you have not learned about that yet in school, you will very soon. Let me give you the two-minute version. I will use an old classic, the lemonade stand as an example.

Before the Industrial Revolution, you sold lemonade the old fashioned way. You set up a stand right in front of your house and sold to a few people that happened to pass by. On average, about eight to twelve people.

Every day, you needed about a gallon of water, 1 ½ cups of lemon juice, 2 cups of sugar, and some ice. Pretty easy. So easy in fact, you can make the lemonade all by yourself. You got your lemons from a neighbor who had a lemon tree. Occasionally, you had to go to a country store to get some sugar.

You didn't have to work too hard, and you had plenty of time to spend time with your family, go to school, and play. You made enough money to have everything you needed. That is how you sold lemonade before the Industrial Revolution.

But then came the Industrial Revolution, and things changed dramatically. There were new lemonade makers popping up everywhere. These new lemonade makers didn't use lemonade stands.

They started making massive amounts of lemonade, which they froze and shipped all over the country. This gave customers the option to buy frozen lemonade, and then take it home and make lemonade whenever they felt the urge.

The cost of this new form of lemonade to the customer was comparable to the price you offered. The quality was not as good as what you produced, but it was more convenient.

To make matters even more difficult for you, some of your customers started buying the new stuff. And your neighbor who sold you lemons, raised his prices and the quality of the lemons were not as good. Why? Because he was selling almost everything he had to the new lemonade makers. The only lemons he sold you were the rejects.

You had two choices. Keep doing lemonade the old fashioned way, or get into the Industrial Revolution game. You chose the game.

In order to compete, you had to mass produce lemonade. Every day you needed about 1,000 gallons of water, 1,500 cups of lemon juice, 2,000 cups of sugar, and boatloads of ice. Making lemonade was no longer easy. You could not do this on your own, so you had to hire some help.

Finding help was not easy. You hired anyone you could find. Most of the people you hired were poor. You hired children as young as 8, and adults as old as 70. You hired females and males. You made all of them work about nine hours a day.

You learned that you could pay adult men about a dime an hour, women a nickel, and children just a few cents. As wrong as that sounds on many levels, everyone else was doing it, so you did too. You had to so that you could sell your lemonade at the same price as the competition. If you didn't, you would have gone out of business.

You worked long hours, and you had little time to spend with your family. But, that was ok. Your family didn't have time for you either. They were all working in your new lemonade factory.

I could go on, but you get the idea. The Industrial Revolution came upon the scene very fast. Many wonderful innovations were developed, but there were many negative consequences too. The working conditions were horrible. There were no rules governing safety practices in factories, or how people that worked in factories should be treated. Those came later.

The workers were mostly poor, and the living they made barely was enough to make it day by day. The factory owners were rich, and they become even richer over the course of the Industrial Revolution. This created a big divide between the wealthy and the poor. H.G. Wells was born on the poor side. He was born a Have-Not.

H.G. Wells grew up to be a Socialist. He believed that wealth and private property could be redistributed to others less fortunate as determined necessary by some organization such as a government. For example, let's assume you live in a Socialist country, and you very successful and become mega-rich.

The government might say, you have too much and we are going to take a lot of your success and give it away to others that are not so successful. You have no say as to whom they give it to or in what form they give away your wealth.

H.G. Wells did not believe in Capitalism, which is what we have in the United States. Capitalism assumes that the very act of doing business will redistribute wealth and property naturally.

For example, imagine a very wealthy person living in a Capitalist country. Let's use Oprah. Oprah is one of the richest women in the world. The government does not take her money away (other than taxes); Oprah gives it away and chooses where her money goes.

One example is her Oprah Winfrey Leadership Academy for Girls in South Africa. This academy is for low-income seventh and eighth graders. Without her generosity, these girls would not have access to this level of education. Some of these girls will grow up and make incredible contributions to the world. Some will probably become very wealthy, and will do something similar with their wealth.

Oprah is planting seeds, and many of those seeds will grow up and make even more seeds. See? You know, it only takes one acorn to make a forest.

H.G. Wells was not a Capitalist. *The Time Machine* was his way of expressing his protest against capitalistic ideals. In his opinion, these ideals led to a society where the rich and powerful could take advantage of those not rich or powerful.

While I don't agree with him, I am fascinated with how he expressed his beliefs through this incredibly creative science fiction novella. Isn't that interesting that these geeky stories and movies classified as science fiction might contain some hidden message?

My Love, you can see hidden messages in everything if you look closely enough, and I encourage you to do just that. We talked about Michelangelo and the brain.

I choose to see a message in the zombie phenomenon. The sun rising after dark has inspired millions of people for as long as there have been people. H.G. Wells wrote several science fiction stories that expressed his beliefs.

And you know that group of ponies that we watch together? Do you know what I see? That people, just like ponies, can be better together because they are different.

Your future is determined by the thoughts that you have in the present.

Would you ever take a vacation to a city dump? Then don't imagine one.

DEAR DAUGHTER, TRAVEL TO THE FUTURE WISELY

Dear Daughter,

You are a time traveler to a future of endless possibilities. We all are! Having the ability to imagine the future is part of who you are.

I have seen you travel to the future many times. You stare off in to space. Your eyes grow glassy and watery, because you don't blink. You are looking, but you aren't seeing the "here and now."

In your mind's eye however, you see something. The question is, "What?" Or maybe the better question is, "How is your time trip making you feel?"

Emotion plays a major role in how your life progresses. Thinking good and hopeful thoughts about the future will result in good feelings now. And, that my little Time Traveler, is a piece of the formula for having an amazing life.

This is as real as gravity. This is law, meaning it is always true.

The machine that you use to journey to the future is called your imagination. The very fact that you have an imagination should be a clue that it is an important part of you, kind of like your heart is an important part of the body. Your imagination is very powerful! When it is used wisely, your imagination can prove to be a very helpful tool in life.

It can also jack you up and your life when used improperly. Of all the subjects in school that should be taught but are not, Imagination 101 could top the list.

Hmmm, maybe that is my job to teach you about your imagination. Scratch that thing I said about schools.

Consider this your first and last lesson. Everything you need to know about traveling in time to the future on "Spaceship Imagination" can be said in minutes. Following what you are about to learn however, is a daily practice. You should do it every single day.

This is not something that you will master, and from that point forward you have it. Your imagination is nothing at all like a bicycle. There will be no, "I'm good. I learned that already."

You know who Einstein is. Now you know that he is the one that proved that you could journey many years in to the future in what felt like a very short time.

To do so, you just have to travel near the speed of light, yes, near that little o' thing, the speed of light.

Einstein, was very smart and knowledgeable about many topics. Yet, he said, "Imagination is more important than knowledge." Wow! Einstein, *the* smarty pants, considered imagination to be more important than knowledge.

"What you imagine determines your life!" That is so important, I will say it once more, "What you imagine determines your life."

It matters just as much as eating the right foods, breathing clean air, and drinking clean water. Seriously, it is the difference between a happy you and a miserable you.

You must wake up every day committed to traveling to good places. You should wake up every day choosing not to travel to nightmare futures.

I have good news for you though. You were born with a built-in navigation warning system. When you are time traveling to a dangerous place, this system will let you know.

Likewise, when you time travel to a wonderful place, your system will let you know that also. There is no user's manual, because it is so easy to learn. Here is how it works.

If thinking about anything in the future stirs emotions that cause you to feel bad, then you are treading into a future where you don't belong.

"What do you think I might be talking about?"

One example is worrying. There is absolutely nothing good that comes from worrying, "Nothing at all." In fact, worrying causes you harm and here's why.

When your body senses danger, it releases some "go-go juice" in your body so you can respond to that danger. People that study this kind of stuff call it "fight or flight" which means your muscles and brain are temporarily amped up so that you can make quick decisions, run like crazy, or fight against the danger. This is just one of the many amazing things your body does.

You might have heard the stories where people showed superhuman strength in times of incredible danger such as moms lifting cars off their children that were trapped underneath. Well, those stories are true, and the reason is because of that "go-go juice."

The problem with worry is that it releases the very same "go-go juice." But, there is a big difference between a dangerous situation happening in the present and worrying about something in the future that is not happening. Pretty obvious, huh? One is now, and the other is in the future.

With dangerous moments happening in the present, the juice stops releasing when the danger has passed. This allows the body to relax and go back into its normal state.

With worrying however, the danger never goes away. And, because it is in the future, there is nothing you can run from.

"There is nothing to fight!"

As long as those worrisome thoughts are there, the "go-go juices" keep pumping. Remaining in that amped up "fight or flight" state for days and days is bad for your body and brain. Not just a little bad, really bad.

"How bad?"

"Toxic bad, as in poisoning your body!"

You will become tense in the muscles that have been put into red alert mode, ready to fire. You will lose sleep, and you will lose your ability to concentrate.

For older people, the risk of heart attacks and strokes goes way up. But, you are a young gun, so let me tell you more about the effects of worry on someone your age.

I just know this will make an example that pops. You might get a zit, one of those really bad ones that makes others think of some red-nosed reindeer whenever they see you.

Of course, it is all about location. The zit could even make you look like a Cyclops. You know, the kind of zit that makes you want to hide. Both still suck.

Now to put this in perspective, worrying does not change the outcome for the good one iota. So, why do it? Don't.

"But Dad, how do I not do that?"

Good question, and as usual, I have an answer.

"Distract yourself."

You must find a way to take your mind off whatever it is that you are worrying about, and put it on silly things. I sometimes make fun of those kitties on the internet and people that spend their time watching them, but they are on to something. It makes them smile, and it puts their minds in a great place.

The internet is full of videos that are so silly, cute, and innocent that you cannot help but smile. If kitties don't do it for you, baby racing is an excellent choice. Practically anything with babies will work.

You also need to move that bootie of yours, as in exercise. Moving your body is like flushing the toilet after number two. It helps get rid of trash your body does not need.

Playing some sport, riding a bike or swimming does wonders for your mind and your body. And, for some reason, it just takes a little while to calm you down.

Once you have stopped worrying for a while, you don't really want to do it anymore. You might even find that you can think about that same worrisome situation in an entirely different way.

You might think about solutions. You might have feelings of hope bubble up. You might realize that no matter what happens, it will be ok.

After all, you are here right now, which means that you have faced many challenging situations. And yet, you are still here. Feeling in any of these ways means you have taken back your power.

"Worrying has no power!"

It places you in a helpless and hopeless state of mind.

Also, you need to be aware of what triggers worry: sad songs, retelling over and over and over and over your sob story to any sad sack that will listen. . .

"Oh paleeze!"

And, for goodness sake, I have said it once, but I will say it again.

"No posting your blankety blankety blankety on the blank!"

I am cussing right now. Posting your story on social media or telling a world that really doesn't have your best interest at heart is not a good idea.

"That will get you blankety blankety blankety!"

I am still cussing. Posting your worry on the internet for the world to see will cause your readers to ask questions, ask more questions, and ask even more questions about what you are going through. And yep, you guessed it. The cycle of worrying starts over.

When you were born, worrying was not something you knew how to do. Worrying was a learned skill. And, "Dag-nabbit!" you probably learned it from me.

I know that on more than one occasion during those infant years, we parents were not as quick to tend to some need you had as you would have liked.

"How do I know this?"

Because, you told us with that wonderful and very effective language.

"Waah waah!"

On those occasions, you weren't saying, "Oh my goodness, oh my goodness! Is that rubbery-feeling thingy that leaks milk ever coming back? Oh my goodness! Oh my goodness! What will I do if that rubbery-thingy never comes back? Hmmm. . . maybe I should try my toe. It is about the same size and shape."

Nope, you were saying, "Get that rubbery-thingy in my mouth right now, cuz I am hungry!"

Don't worry my little time traveling princess, I am done talking about worry.

"Hardy har har." Clever dad made a joke.

Now let's talk about some fun time traveling.

"After all, feeling good and having fun is the purpose of life.

Right?

So where in the future might we travel that serves that purpose

Daydreaming is a blast. Look at a magazine or watch a show about some cool place that tickles your desire. It could be the moon, the ocean, the mountains, a hot-air balloon. . . anything. Then spend a little time creating a movie in your head that is awesome, fun, and adventurous about you experiencing the inspirational place or activity. Your imagination can create some incredible movies.

"You will feel really good!"

Visualization is a blast. Sometimes, you will have some important event coming up that you can't stop thinking about. It could be a game, a test, or maybe a trip. Whatever it is, you are thinking about it more than other things. So, make a movie how that event occurs.

You need to be a little careful with visualization. It can be tricky. If you get too specific with your thoughts, you might find yourself struggling to create your movie. For example, let's say you have a big test tomorrow. You have studied and you feel ready but you still can't stop thinking about it. This is called anxiety.

It might be hard for you to create a movie in your mind that shows you whizzing through the test and not missing a single question.

On the other hand, you will find it much easier to see yourself taking the test, feeling relaxed, feeling confident, smiling, and nodding as you answer the questions, flipping the pages of the test with a snap of confidence, and then turning it in to the teacher and feeling very good about how you did.

"See? That is more general, and easier for you to think through and believe!"

Inventing is a blast. Every invention, was first created in the imagination by someone. During your lifetime, you will encounter gadgets or processes that just seem ridiculously inefficient. You will say to yourself, "There has to be a better way."

Seize those moments my little inventor, and imagine that "better way." Every invention starts in your imagination. It does not matter if you know how to create your invention. The world is full of resources. Someone will know how to fill in the missing pieces.

Sweetheart, even though I know you are going to turn up your nose, I do hope you find some time to check out the science fiction genre. But that is not nearly as important as taking your own trips to the future and writing your own wonderful and fun stories.

And just to let you know, your trips to the future are technically science fiction.

You are the author of your life. Life does not happen to you. It happens because of you. Take control of your thoughts and choose thoughts that support the purpose of your life, and you will be very happy. "I promise!"

Love,

Dad

KEY 6

Having a Life Full of Miracles

- "Lluvia de Peces," The Rain of Fish
- Dear Daughter, Believe in Miracles

This is an engraving from the 1500's, created by Olaus Magnus. Engravings are created by cutting into a flat surface to create an image.

The image depicts fish falling from the sky.

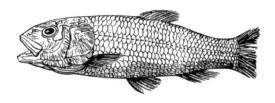

"LLUVIA DE PECES," THE RAIN OF FISH

I n the last chapter, we talked about using your imagination to time travel to the future. We also talked about how important it is that you only travel to a future that stirs within you good feelings.

This is so important, that I am tempted to say it twice.

It is really, really, really important that you only time travel to a future that stirs within you those good feelings.

Listen my little wonder, your thoughts are like GPS for your life. The reason I keep bringing this up is because it is both true and important. Your life will navigate in whatever direction you believe. Would you prefer a life replete with miracles, or "bad luck?"

Speaking of miracles, I want to share with you a very amazing story. While it may seem fishy, and trust me it will, this story is true. This is a story about fish raining down from the sky.

More than 150 years ago, the Catholic Church in Spain ordered a priest to leave his home, and sail almost halfway around the world to a tiny village in Honduras called Yoro.

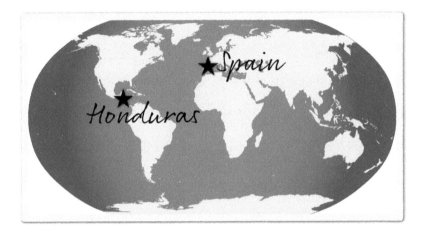

This was not a vacation, Niña.

Yoro was a very poor place at that time.

The people barely had enough food to eat. The homes were tiny shacks. The roofs leaked. If it was hot outside, it was hotter inside their tiny homes. A toilet was nothing more than a hole in the ground.

There was no privacy. Everyone heard each other's farts, burps, laughs and cries. And not everyone living in homes were people.

I am remembering a song from my childhood days. It is one I have heard you sing as well. I am talking about the old classic "Old McDonald Had a Farm."

With a cluck cluck here
And a cluck cluck there
Here a cluck, there a cluck
Everywhere a cluck cluck
With a baa baa here
And a baa baa there
Here a baa, there a baa
Everywhere a baa baa
With a neigh neigh here
And a neigh neigh there
Here a neigh, there a neigh
Everywhere a neigh neigh
With a quack quack here
And a quack quack there
Here a quack, there a quack
Everywhere a quack quack
With a oink oink here
And a oink oink there
Here a oink, there a oink
Everywhere a oink oink
With a moo moo here
And a moo moo there
Here a moo, there a moo
Everywhere a moo moo

Old MacDonald had a farm
E-I-E-I-OOOOOOO

Can you imagine sharing your home with any of them?

The Catholic Church has sent people to far off places like this
for many hundreds of years. It is kind of their "thang." They
focus a great deal on helping those that are suffering, usually

from poverty. The individuals that are chosen to travel so that they can help others in need, their sacrifices are enormous.

Can you imagine if someone said, "Hey Padre, 'wassup?' I need you to pack your bags. You are boarding a boat next week, and you will sail across the ocean for about 8 weeks.

"Then you will be escorted by soldiers for about 200 miles to a place called Yoro. You will be riding a horse. The people who you are going to stay with don't speak the same language or eat the same foods as you do.

"In fact, they share nothing in common with you except that they are people. And, they don't even know you are coming, so there's that.

"But you can persuade them to let you in and trust you. By the way, they are really poor, which is why we are sending you. Okay?"

The people that are sent on such missions are called missionaries. The lucky one sent to Yoro more than 150 years ago, was named Father Jose Manuel Subirana.

Father Jose Manuel Subirana is a mouthful, so from now on we will call him Padre. Yoro was Padre's final home, he died in Yoro.

Ok, so we have this place called Yoro. Times were tough! People were hungry and poor. Padre was thousands of miles from his home, living in Yoro.

As the story is told today by the people of Yoro, Padre had compassion for the people in Yoro. He lived with and loved them like family.

According to the story, Padre was so moved by the suffering of the people, that he prayed for three days and three nights for God to give these people some sign of hope.

Dude was seeking a miracle, and a miracle he received.

Shortly after this three-day outreach to God, a rain fell. Now rains fall in Honduras in the months of May, June, and July with regularity, so that was no miracle. But, what rained on this particular day was very different. On that day, it rained fish.

When the rain stopped, the people went out into the streets and noticed that the streets were covered with many thousands of tiny fish. The hungry people gathered make-shift buckets, and filled them full of the fish that fell from the sky. Then, the people of Yoro cooked those tiny fish and ate to their heart's content. There was plenty for everyone.

Now here is the interesting part. These fish have fallen in Yoro a day or two every year during the rainy season, since it first happened. Every single year, the fish have fallen.

In fact, this tiny village now has an annual festival with a parade and all, called "Lluvia de Peces," translated as "Rain of the Fishes."

Attending that festival is definitely on my bucket list.

No one has been able to explain this phenomenon, but there are many theories. Some think that the water spouts and wind pick the fish up during the storm and drop them off in the valley where these people live. The explanation is probably something like that, but they can't seem to figure out where the fish come from, or why it started in the first place.

Listen my little "Princessa," what I am about to say is "mucho importante." All miracles, or nearly all miracles, have some scientific explanation. And that does not matter one hill of beans.

A miracle is still a miracle, whether it can be explained or not. Someday someone with a lot of letters after their name is going to explain the Yoro miracle. In some weird accent with a voice that sounds like their butt cheeks are pinched tighter than a snare drum, they will say something like this.

"The Yoro phenomenon is no miracle at all. The Yoro phenomenon is nothing more than the coalescing of repeatable atmospheric conditions with a change in the location of the spawning of a freshwater, underground fish that is indigenous to that region; their previous spawning location was compromised due to a geological disturbance caused by the mining of...."

"Blah, blah, blah."

We humans are funny. Most of us don't really take a liking to things that can't be explained. It makes us feel uncomfortable. And because of this, those uncomfortable people breathe a big sigh of relief once a so-called miracle is explained. DON'T be one of those people.

You are a miracle!

The way the planets float in space, spinning around our sun year after year – miraculous. The water cycle – miracle. The perfect balance in nature that would fall apart if there were no more bees, sharks, worms or other things that you don't like – miracle. I could go on and on.

Miracles are everywhere. All you have to do to experience them is open your eyes and heart, and believe that anything is possible. Do this, and miracles will be a common occurrence in your life.

It will make your amazing life, even more amazing!

And if someone "smart" comes along and offers an explanation for a miracle, pat that person on the back. It is well deserved! However, their explanation in no way takes away the miracle. In a way, their explanation gives more credence to the miracle.

Be in awe of the universe and the events that happen in your life. There are miracles happening every day.

Keep your eyes and heart open, and you will see them.

DEAR DAUGHTER, BELIEVE IN MIRACLES

Dear Daughter,

Do you remember the day when we planted a seed in a jar? We filled that jar up with soil, and planted that seed smack dab in the middle of that soil about a half-inch deep. We sprinkled a little water on the top of the soil. We placed the jar outside in the backyard, where we knew our seed would get a lot of sun. You were 4 at that time. We were both very excited.

About five minutes later, I heard the door chime go off, and I knew you had gone back outside. I rushed through the house to investigate, and I noticed the back door was standing wide open. I walked up to the door and looked outside, and there you were.

You were bending over and looking into our jar, with your hands supported by your knees. You wanted to see if our little seedling had popped out. I smile and laugh every time I think about that image. It was so darn cute! You were looking for the miracle that you knew was coming, although five minutes was a touch too soon. But, you knew it was coming.

When you were about 9, I took you to a far off island in the Pacific. We went snorkeling one day on a reef where the fish are as colorful as rainbows. You had never seen fish like the ones that were swimming in the reef beneath us, nor had I.

I remember you putting your head underwater to gaze into the beauty beneath. I put my head underwater too. You were excited to see whatever you could see. You were looking with expectation. You had no doubt that you would see some amazing fish.

Within seconds, your arms starting moving around uncontrollably under the water. I could hear your voice screaming through your mouthpiece. I couldn't understand a word you were saying, but I understood the emotion.

We both poked our heads out of the surface. You relaxed your mouth around that snorkel but you didn't take it out of your mouth because you were too excited. You screamed with joy, knowing that you had just seen a miracle.

"I thaw a fith! I thaw a fith!"

Of course, you meant to say, "I saw a fish!"

I saw that rainbow fish too, among many other colorful fish. But that rainbow fish that was so close to you was splendid to behold.

So, what is a miracle exactly? If you ask a thousand people, you will you will get a thousand, very personal and very different stories. You will not get a definition. You will get stories.

You will hear of visits to breathtaking oceans, mountains, or canyons. You will hear about sunsets and sunrises. You will hear amazing stories of healing. Some will talk about microscopic miracles, while others will talk about the macroscopic universe.

There will be stories about how someone survived a lightning strike, and gained special powers not had before. You will hear about visions and dreams. You will hear about encounters with loved ones that have passed away.

There will be stories of near-missed catastrophes. There will be stories of angels and God. And, you will hear stories about signs, such as the story that the people of Yoro so passionately tell to this day. And my sweetheart, you are a miracle. There isn't a day that goes by that I don't know that.

Here are other interesting observations about miracles. Two people can share a certain experience at the very same moment, and one will experience a miracle while the other will not.

And a person can see the sunset for days upon days, but then suddenly there comes one day when they see that sunset as a miracle.

There are some people who insist that miracles must be magical, and impossible to explain. The religious leaders during Michelangelo's time were in this camp.

Remember?

They were the "science is a no-no" guys. They feared that if the miracle could be explained by science, then the belief in the miracle would go away.

With so many miracle stories from so many people, it is difficult to put in to words exactly what a miracle is. When I struggle with being able to explain with words, something that I know in my heart, I sometimes go back to the origin of the word itself.

What did this word mean when it first became part of language?

By the way, studying the origin of words is referred to as etymology. On the other hand, the study of bugs is known as entomology. Studying the origin of the word bugs is not called "ety-entomology." That is still etymology.

The word miracle comes from the Latin root, "mirari" which meant "to wonder at." "Wonder" is a bit of an odd word in itself. According to the dictionary gods, "wonder" is that feeling when you mix surprise, beauty and admiration at the same time.

Here is a bit of trivia for you. The word mirror comes from the very same Latin root, "mirari." Ok, "backus" to the Latin origins of the word miracle.

A miracle is an experience that stirs within, a feeling of surprise, because the experience was unexpected.

A miracle is an experience that causes one to see beauty and goodness at that moment.

A miracle is an experience that stirs within, feelings of admiration and awe.

Do you notice what is going on here? Those Latin speakers don't talk at all about specific experiences. They talk about emotions. They talk about feelings. They talk about several specific feelings experienced at the same time.

People cannot tell you what a miracle is. They can only tell you about an experience that they believe was a miracle.

All the different miracle stories that are told by people have one thing in common. Those stories express the feelings that each miracle beholder experienced! How cool is that? A miracle is an emotional bomb that is triggered by a single event that just so happens to have a whole lot to do with that person's life at that very moment.

My child, life is going to present you plenty of opportunities to experience miracles. But it is up to you, to see them. Every night when you go to bed, let go of the challenges that you are experiencing. No matter how big those challenges may seem at that moment, they are not too big for you and the Power within you. They are not too big for a miracle.

And don't spend your time trying to figure out the details on how things are going to work out. Just get to that place of belief that everything is working out for you in the best of ways. And when you wake up in the morning, take a few moments before you pop out of bed to reconnect with that belief. Start and end your days like this.

And then go throughout your day with the same expectation you showed with the seed we planted together. Dive into the day knowing that you are about to see a rainbow fish, and you will see rainbows and rainbow fish at exactly the right time.

Do this, and miracles will happen for you big and small. And when they do, take the time to acknowledge those miracles and say thanks. You might even keep a log of miracles. We people are funny; we tend to forget the blessings we receive.

Love,

Dad

KEY 7

Understanding Your Eternal Nature

— Water
— Dear Daughter, You are Like Water

About 71 percent of the Earth's surface is water. 96.5 percent of the water is in the salty oceans. More than half of your body is water.

When scientists search for life on other planets, they look for signs of water.

But there is more to water. Water tells stories of unconditional cleansing, resurrection, and eternity.

WATER

In the last chapter, we talked about "The Rain of Fish" miracle of Yoro, Honduras. I thought this would be the perfect time to talk to you about water, and why we have rain. Specifically, I want to tell you about a miracle known as the water cycle. This is going to flood your mind with thoughts, I just know it.

The earth is old. Really, really, really old. More than four billion years old. That number is so big you can't even imagine it. You know how long a year is. Birthdays and summer and Christmas have tuned you in to what a year feels like.

You might even be able to grasp 1,000 years because of your history classes. But four billion, no way. One billion is one thousand million. The earth is o-l-d.

Just as it is today, when the earth became earth long ago, there was water. Would you believe me if I told you that the amount of water on the earth then, and the amount of water today is the same? Tis true.

Not only is the amount the same, but the water is the same. Yep, the water you drink is prehistoric, more than 4 billion years old. The water you drink today, most likely quenched the thirsts of many other living creatures from long ago.

How is that possible? What is going on here? The water cycle, that's what.

Most of the water on this beautiful planet is salt water. In fact, about 97% of the water is salty, and you can't drink that stuff. About 2% of the water is frozen in glaciers at the North and South Poles. You can't drink that either, because you can't travel to the poles. And even if you could, you can't drink ice.

So how much does that leave for drinking, flushing yucky stuff down toilets, taking soapy baths and showers, washing dirty clothes, washing cars, and your favorite thing to do of all, washing dirty dishes? 1%. Just 1% of the water on this planet is fresh water that you can use. Holy thundercloud, that is not very much.

Without the water cycle, it would not take long for that 1% of the earth's water to become a soup of soap, poop, pee, dirt, toxic waste, and soggy old food. Yuck!

So, what is this miracle known as the water cycle, and how does it work? Well my little raindrop, here is how.

The water cycle has four main processes that "flow" from one to the next in an endless loop. Those four processes are called collection, evaporation, condensation, and precipitation.

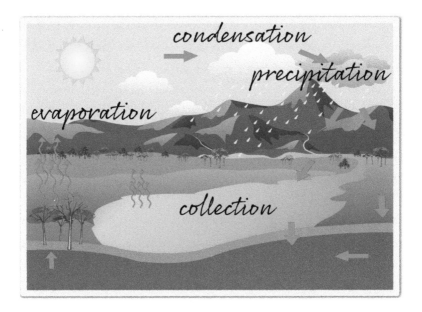

The water cycle is a bit like the "chicken and the egg" conundrum. We don't really have a starting place. For our discussion, let's first look at the collection process.

The collection process is when water is gathered into pools, puddles, lakes, rivers, salty oceans, and sewers.

That last one, the sewers, are where the yuckiest water collects. That is where the water from sinks and toilets flow. It is also where the dirty water on the street goes after a rain. If you drink sewage water, it will make you barf. Stay out of sewers.

The next part of the water cycle is evaporation.

This is my favorite.

The heat of the sun shines down on the collected water, and changes it into a gas which rises into the air. It is still water, but the form has changed from a liquid to a gas.

The cool thing is, that when the water evaporates, it leaves all the sewer muck, dirt and salt behind. Only water is lifted into the air in the form of a gas, called water vapor.

The next process in the water cycle is condensation. When the water vapor rises high into the air, the vapor starts to get cold and the gas starts to turn back into liquid by forming tiny drops of water. When you see clouds, you are seeing just that.

This is the same thing that is happening when you have a glass with something cold to drink in it. The water vapor in the air starts to get cold around the glass, and turns back into water. This is why your glass gets wet on the outside. Pretty cool stuff.

Clouds are formed when water vapor starts to change back into liquid or ice. In a cloud, the water is condensing into millions of teensy tiny drops, or pieces of ice if it is cold enough.

Initially, clouds are white. But when a lot of water vapor starts to condense in a cloud, the color changes to gray.

Well, what goes up must come down. The last part of the water cycle is precipitation. Eventually, the water in the clouds becomes too much to remain in the air. The water droplets or the ice crystals fall back down to the ground in the form of rain, sleet, snow, or hail. This is called precipitation.

Now where do you think the water or ice falling down lands? Some of it lands on the ground, but most of it lands in the ocean, lakes, rivers, streams, and ponds. In other words, it collects.

And then the whole water cycle starts over again, and just as before, the yuck is left behind during the evaporation process.

Isn't that cool? I know it happens every day, but try to see the marvelous in the familiar. The Designer of this whole universe is brilliant! This is one of those miracles that is worth acknowledging.

I want to close by sharing with you a story about the country Bermuda. Yes, that Bermuda, as in the Bermuda Triangle. Bermuda is a tiny island in the Atlantic Ocean. When I say tiny, I mean twenty square miles tiny. That is smaller than most of the cities in America, and Bermuda is a country.

You might not know this, but most of us get our water from underground pools of water called aquifers.

There is no natural water in Bermuda. Bermuda depends entirely on rain which they catch in buckets as it drains off their roofs. People have lived in Bermuda since the early 1600's. Bermudians have no problem appreciating the water cycle for the miracle that it is. If there was any lengthy drought, all the people there would have moved on from this world. Talk about faith.

Nothing on this planet is wasted.
After something dies, the physical
stuff is not destroyed. Instead, it
is transformed back into the very
matter that gives way to the
creation of new life.

The life-force energy that is
"you," is no different. Your spirit
is also transformed, and reunited
with God.

DEAR DAUGHTER, YOU ARE LIKE WATER

Dear Daughter,

Water is the most amazing, yet most unappreciated substance on this planet. I have barely made a ripple in the vast oceans of knowledge there is about water.

I am on a roll here with puns and stuff.

Now that you have expanded your appreciation of the water cycle miracle, let's go further. You and water have so much in common.

Water has three forms, solid, liquid, and vapor. All of them are necessary for life here on earth.

You might not know this, but any of those three forms can exist at the same time on every single day of the year. Take a glass of ice water, and walk outside and look for clouds. Clouds are not water vapor, but they are formed from water vapor. On any given day and in every part of this world, you can walk outside and see all three forms of water at the same time. Water is the only compound on earth that can make such a claim.

When I reflect upon the three forms of water, I find myself thinking about how you and I also have three forms. Water comes in ice, liquid, and vapor. You and I have a body, a mind, and a spirit.

I can hear you now. "Dad, what are you talking about?" Stick with me love. By the end of this, it will all make sense.

When water freezes, each water molecule slows way down and joins to multiple other water molecules in different directions and angles, and they stay joined. In a way, they are like "besties," as long as the temperature is below freezing.

This is how snowflakes are formed.

Ice is some powerful stuff. It has carved the earth like a giant buzz saw running wild. Many of the valleys across the world as well as the small ponds and lakes, were created by slow-moving glaciers.

When water seeps into cracks within rocks and then freezes, it can break that rock apart with ease. I am not talking just about little rocks. Entire sides of mountains have been sheered off like sliced cake, from freezing water. *If ice could be added to the rock, paper scissors game, ice would never lose.*

The potholes in the street are there because water seeped into cracks in the street and then froze.

You see, water expands when it freezes. Most of the other substances on this planet don't do that. This by the way, is the reason why ice floats!

Ice at the North and South Poles serve a very important purpose for the entire planet, including the sunny parts. Believe it or not, it keeps our weather and seasons balanced. Without those ice caps at the poles, the weather would go crazy all over the world.

"Ok dad, so what does all of this ice talk have to do with me?"

"Sweet daughter, you seem to always ask things at exactly the right time. And that really helps me with my transitions... keep it up!"

The ice form of water is like the physical form of you. By that, I mean the part of you that interacts with the physical world. And just like ice, this part of you is powerful. Your actions carve up your world like a buzz saw.

Meet someone new? Everything changes. Smile or frown at someone? Everything changes. Do your homework or not? Everything changes. Say something nice or mean? Everything changes. Take action or take no action? Everything changes.

Ok my little snowflake, let's talk about another one of water's forms. Let's talk about liquid water.

When liquid water moves upon the land or underneath the ground, it always takes the path of least resistance.

Hmmm.

The walls of the Grand Canyon are not straight, and the shores of puddles, ponds, lakes, and oceans are not round. Water erodes the earth where it is easiest.

Liquid water is necessary for plants, animals, and you to stay alive.

Kind of important.

Moving water has enormous energy, which we have learned to convert into electricity.

Liquid water is "faster" than ice. The molecules in liquid water are moving around way too fast to bond into ice, but not so fast that they all break apart into a vapor. And just like ice, the impact of liquid water upon the world is enormous.

"Ok dad, I understand what you said about ice. But what does all of this liquid water talk have to do with me?"

"Daughter, I am so glad you asked. You always ask the right questions at exactly the right time"

The liquid form of water is like your mind, in constant fluid motion. When running water runs into an obstacle, there is resistance. When that obstacle is encountered, the flow of water changes course to get past the resistance. Sometimes there is no path, in which case the water continues to collect until the obstacle is overwhelmed, like when a dam breaks.

Many of the choices you make and the beliefs you hold are doing the same thing, navigating around obstacles. And just like water, your mind is programmed to find the path of least resistance.

But, of course, you won't always follow the path of least resistance. Sometimes, you will find yourself making choices that have the most resistance. It's called free will. Yep, we all have the free will to be stubborn, prideful and to make things harder on ourselves than they have to be.

When you use your mind for daydreaming, pretending, playing, imagining, finding solutions, inventing or anything creative, you feel alive. You are flowing like a river.

When you use your mind for condemning, feeling hopeless, feeling sorry for yourself, thinking how unfair life is, and all that other yucky stuff, you feel stagnant.

We use the word stagnant to describe a body of water that has no flow, and thus becomes stinky and full of bacteria. What a perfect word to describe a mind that has no flow.

Like rushing water, the thoughts in your mind have immense energy and creative power. Everything you experience in the physical world, first started as thought.

Your smartphone, your clothes, the house you live in, the car I drive, the mailbox, your school, your toys... anything and everything manmade started first as the thought of some person.

The same is true for the natural world. The planets, suns, oceans, grains of sand, trees, cockroaches, lobsters, volcanoes, rats, comets, moons... anything and everything that is not manmade started first as a thought of God.

Before I continue, I need to make sure you understand something. The mind is not the brain. Ok? The brain is an organ where a lot of nervous system functions take place. Your mind uses the brain, but your mind is not the brain.

Said another way, a car is a vehicle that sits there with all kind of capabilities. Let's call the car the brain. What you choose to do with that car, let's call the mind. You can go here or there. You can drive carefully, or recklessly. You can take shortcuts, or scenic routes. You get the idea. *Michelangelo is smiling right now.*

Ok my little dewdrop. Let's talk about water vapor.

Water vapor is the "fastest" of water's 3 forms. The water molecules are moving so fast in fact, that the water can no longer stay together. The water molecules break apart and are transformed into the unseen form of water vapor.

Water vapor is pure. There are no remnants of the sludge present in the water's other forms. No salt, poop, pee, soap, oil, dirt or germs. All that stuff is left behind, when water is transformed into vapor from the heat of the sun. Without water vapor, this planet would be dead.

Water vapor is like your spirit form. Your spirit is pure and perfect love, and free of "sludge." I am not talking about the salt, poop, pee, soap, oil, dirt, and germs sludge that has no place in water vapor. Your spirit form is devoid of a completely different type of sludge, the type of sludge that cannot coexist with perfect love.

⁴Love is patient, love is kind. It does not envy, it does not boast, it is not proud. ⁵It does not dishonor others, it is not self-seeking, it is not easily angered, it keeps no record of wrongs. ⁶Love does not delight in evil but rejoices with the truth. ⁷It always protects, always trusts, always hopes, always perseveres.
(New International Version, 1 Corinthians 13.4-7).

Dang, that is some beautiful stuff.

If love is patient, then impatience must be sludge. If love is kind, then meanness and cruelty must also be sludge. To dishonor means to humiliate or bring shame... definitely sludge. I bet you did not know that worry was sludge. Having judgmental thoughts about yourself or others... yucky sludge. Prejudice and bigotry because of skin color, gender, or any other groupings of people... barf sludge. Celebrating evil acts against others is very scary sludge.

No matter how big or little you think the sludge is, your spirit will have no part of it. Sludge is sludge.

Well then, if your spirit will have nothing to do with sludge, then what part of you does? Your mind part. The physical you definitely carries out many of your sludgy actions, but the mind is where they all start.

Now here is some secret sauce for you. Does any of that sludge feel good? Nope. Do you know why? Because your spirit and your mind are not on the same page. The fact that it does not feel good is in a way, helpful. It is a sign, letting you know that you are off course. It is you telling you to work through things, and get past it.

This is so important for you to understand, love. You see, the creative power of the mind is the same no matter what types of thoughts you choose. This includes those sludgy thoughts fueled by stubbornness and pride.

When your mind and spirit are not on the same page and you feel bad, this is your spirit form screaming at your mind to stop thinking those sludgy thoughts. Otherwise, those negative thoughts will start to create a string of negative events in your life. Heed the warning signs and get your mind back in synch with your spirit as soon as you can.

The longer you keep thinking sludge, the longer you will continue to feel bad and have negative experiences. Some people are so stubborn, that they have lived their entire earthly life in a war with themselves and with the people around them. You know people like this. Their life is full of one bad event after another.

Sweetheart, you are eternal. Though one day, your body will no longer live, your spirit will live forever. While you are here on this earth however, your spirit keeps cleaning you up from sludge.

No matter what mistakes you might make throughout your life, your spirit part of you never looks at those mistakes. Your spirit part of you never judges you, or thinks of you in a bad way. Your spirit part of you, your soul, only sees you as perfect. This part of you is God, living inside of you.

Love, to bring this to a conclusion, I have just a few last pieces of advice. Question everything, and be aware of how you feel. The wonderful truth about life is, you get to choose. During that process, notice your feelings. As for the beliefs you hold, question those too. Some of those beliefs might not be serving you well.

Imagine back to the time when you first experienced a gushy puppy. As a toddler, that experience was wonderful for you. That puppy grunted and whimpered. That puppy wagged its tail with excitement. That puppy was warm and soft. That puppy licked your face with its stinky puppy breath. You laughed and laughed.

Now just for grins, imagine that puppy biting you on the nose and causing you to bleed. In this scenario, you might form a belief that all puppies are bad. That would be unfortunate. Think of how much joy puppies bring.

If a belief has the word always, never, all, or none, then that belief probably is a bit off. The truth is, most puppies you meet are wonderful. And yes, there are a few out there that might hurt you. The same is true with everything.

You are finding your way love just perfectly. I love watching you grow in every way.

Love,

Dad

PART 4

Having Fun Together
With Activities

CREATING A DREAM POUCH

ACTIVITY TYPE

This is an art project, combined with a bit of good habit forming. We are both going to make a dream pouch, incorporating some of Michelangelo's hidden-secret techniques.

I bet you can guess what we are going to place inside of our dream pouch. Yep, you guessed it. Dreams.

By the way, Michelangelo wasn't the only one that hid secrets within his creations. You can find secrets in music, art, architecture, the layouts of cities, books, poetry, currency, newspapers, languages and more.

SUPPLIES FOR BOTH OF US

• 2 9×12 or 10×13 large mailing envelopes, preferably white

• art supplies of any kind. Crayons, pens, pencils, charcoal, paint, glue, scissors, glitter, stamps, sticky letters and numbers, stickers, yarn, markers, chalk... anything

• 1 can of spray sealant or varnish, used for protecting paintings

• 2 packages of 3×5 index cards

INSTRUCTIONS FOR BOTH OF US

1) Decorate the envelope face. The face is the side without the clasp. Make sure that your artistic embellishments contain references to things that matter to you and that you are passionate about. Taking a cue from Michelangelo, hide at least one of your passions within your artistic design.

2) Once completed, allow your newly created dream pouch to dry.

3) Lightly coat with the sealant and set aside for several hours.

4) It is now time to fill your dream pouch with dreams. Every day, when a desire flashes across your mind, write it on an index card along with the date. *You have these flashes every day, but usually they are forgotten. Let's try to change that.*

5) When you are able, place your dream cards inside your envelope. Right before you do however, read your card once more, and spend about 30 seconds thinking about it. Try to create an emotional response using your very powerful imagination. Make sure that your "dreams" only include what you want. No "don't wants" allowed. Try to keep this up for at least several months. A year, even better. A lifetime would be best.

6) Occasionally, take the time to pull out your dream cards and read them. I think you will be amazed.

WHY THIS MATTERS

All people are natural born thrill seekers. But as people grow older, there is a tendency to lose that quality. They dream less, spending much of their time preparing for the next bad event to occur. What once was a "good day" because something wonderful happened, becomes a "good day" because nothing "bad" happened.

Gosh, that is so sad.

Don't let this happen to you. Stay focused on what you want out of your life.

If you choose to think about what you want out of life, then you will have an amazing life. If you choose to think about what you do not want out of life, then you will have a life full of frustration.

If you choose to not think at all, then you will feel like you have no control over your life. You will feel like a pinball.

Daughter, this life you have is a gift. Treat that gift like the invaluable treasure that it is.

Your thinking patterns are habits. If you find yourself in a negative rut, you may have formed a habit – a bad habit. But you can easily change that. Pay attention to the way you think, and use your power to make choices that serve you instead of hinder you.

When you take the time to revisit your dream pouch, you will notice that many of your dreams came true. You might be tempted to say, "That was just a coincidence," or "That would have happened anyway." Don't say that. Instead, say "Thank you."

You will also notice that some of your dreams did not come true, but many of those dreams you no longer desire. This is perfectly fine. Consider it a good thing that they did not happen. Say "Thank you."

There will be some dreams that came true, but in a completely different and better way than you imagined. Say "Thank you."

And finally, there will be some unfulfilled dreams that are still very much alive in your heart. Keep them alive and trust the process. Prayers are answered in the time that is best, not the time that you think is best. You don't have insight in that timing. God does. Say "Thank you."

My love, everything is working out for you in the best way possible. Trust that.

Love,

Dad

ZOMBIFYING THE BEAUTIFUL

ACTIVITY TYPE

This is an art project, designed to make the beautiful ugly. "What dad? Why?" *Just for fun, sweetheart.* This activity will also raise your awareness about "stinking thinking" choices that transform beautiful people into ugly zombies.

If given the choice, you would prefer to be beautiful, right? Guess what? You have that choice.

We are going to "zombify" a picture of ourselves. Then, we are going to create a before-and-after poster, using the original picture and the zombified version.

SUPPLIES FOR BOTH OF US

• 2 of the same photos of your face (and mine), preferably size 8×10

• 2 poster boards

• 2 fine tip markers, any color

• 1 broad tip marker, any color

• Some eye makeup, lipstick, watercolors, or any other material that can be applied to the photos

INSTRUCTIONS FOR BOTH OF US

1) Set one of the pictures aside. This picture will not be zombified.

2) Take the other picture and make the eyes red. *I used lipstick.*

3) Go around the eyes with a darker color such as dark purple, gray, or blue. *I used eye shadow.*

4) Smear the dark color all around so that it is transparent and looks natural.

5) Color the lips dark, and then spread a little red on top. Try to take away the smile, if there is one. Make a little blood drip out of one of the corners of the mouth.

6) Smear the lips a little to blend the colors. This does not have to be transparent.

7) Make some cuts on the head and anywhere else you want with red or purple. Don't be afraid to pile colors on top of one another.

8) Continue embellishing, making more cuts, bruises, or dark spots wherever desired. How are the photos looking? Zombified? If not, keep working on it.

9) Once done, set the pictures aside to dry. Then spray a light coat of the spray sealant used in the last activity. Set aside for several more hours.

10) Draw a line in the middle of the poster boards from top to bottom, with the broad tip marker.

11) On the top left, write the word "Me" with the broad tip marker.

12) On the top right, write the words "Zombified Me" with the broad tip marker.

13) Glue the untouched photo a few inches below the word "Me" on the left.

14) Glue the zombified photo a few inches below the words "Zombified Me" on the right.

15) A few inches below the photos, drawn 10 lines from left to right across the poster board. Make the lines equally spaced from top to bottom.

16) On the first line on the left, write "1. I can't change the past, so leave it alone and focus on today." On the first line on the right, write "1. Think over and over about something from the past that hurt."

17) On the second line on the left, write "2. Accept responsibility for every choice I have made." On the second line on the right, write "2. Blame others for any hurtful experience I have ever had."

18) On the third line on the left, write "3. Make today better, by learning from past experiences." On the third line on the right, write "3. Regret something I did, and think my life is ruined."

19) On the fourth line on the left, write "4. Forgive others, even if they never say sorry." On the fourth line on the right, write "4. Keep track of all the wrongs that I think others have done."

20) On the fifth line on the left, write "5. Hope for the best. If I can't express hope right now, be quiet until I can." On the fifth line on the right, write "5. Complain all the time, and try to make others feel bad like me."

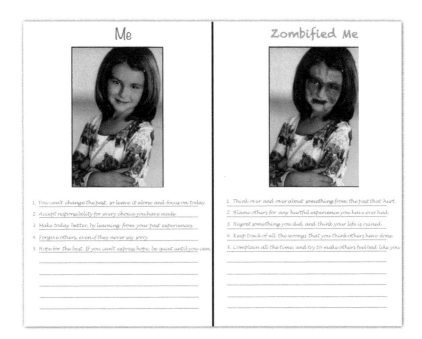

21) Hang your poster in your room, or in a place where you will see it every day.

22) Whenever you discover yourself making a "zombie" choice, write that choice on the right side of your poster. Whenever you discover yourself making a "beautiful" choice, write that choice on the left side of your poster.

WHY THIS MATTERS

The past is a trap for the emotional part of you. For your body, not so much. Touch a hot stove that is glowing red, and I promise you will never do it again. Smell the sweet fragrance of honeysuckle, and I promise you will do it again. You don't have to think about those memories every day to learn from them. You just know. But your emotional self just doesn't "get it."

You will be tempted to replay painful memories over and over. You will be tempted to hold on to grudges toward others. These temptations will get you burned. My darling daughter, there is no need to keep reliving the experience that caused you pain.

Don't get stuck on anything from the past. You can't change it. Getting stuck on past experiences is about the most illogical, dumb thing you could do.

Actually, there is one that is worse. There are some people that repeatedly put themselves back into the very same situation that caused them pain. It is very sad.

Appreciate the past. Without it, you would not be you. And even if you don't feel good about you today, the past is always working in your favor. But for goodness sake, don't give life to what is dead.

Love,

Dad

THE "WHAT WE WANT" CHALLENGE

ACTIVITY TYPE

This is a challenge game, designed to help us learn to focus our thoughts on what you want, instead of what you do not want. *This is a deceptively difficult challenge, sweetheart.* You will be shocked at the amount of attention you give to what you do not want to experience in your life. This exercise will help you change that.

SUPPLIES FOR BOTH OF US

• 1 large piece of paper or poster board

• Some markers, any colors

INSTRUCTIONS

1) Draw a line down the middle of the poster board from top to bottom. Across the top of the poster board, write the following words: "The 'What We Want' Challenge."

2) On the top left, write "Dad Don'ts" and on the top right, write your name followed by the word "Don'ts."

3) Write down the left-hand sign "Day 1," "Day 2," "Day 3," "Day 4," "Day 5," "Day 6," and "Day 7." Draw horizontal lines from left to right, under each of the days.

THE RULES FOR BOTH OF US

1) For one week, avoid using the phrases "I do not want" or "I don't want." Instead, you are going to use the phrase "I want."

2) Every time the phrase "I do not want" or "I don't want" is used, that person gets a mark.

3) At the end of the seven days, the person with the most marks has to take the other person to get ice cream. The one with the most money has to pay! *That would be me, of course.*

EXAMPLES

"Daddy, I want to go get some cheese fries!"

"Daughter, I don't want cheese fries!"

Boo, hiss. Dad gets a mark.

"I want some jalapeño poppers! Is there a place that has both?"

Yippee! No mark. Good job, Dad!

WHY THIS MATTERS

Honey, this little challenge is going to make a big difference in your life. Learning to turn your attention toward what you want keeps your life moving.

When you focus on what you don't want, you put up walls and obstacles. Life will feel like quicksand. Your interactions with others will become argumentative and very frustrating.

When you focus on what you want, your interactions with others becomes easy. Solutions are explored, and everyone "wins." And honestly, it just feels better then fighting.

Obviously, there will be times when the phrases "I do not want" or "I don't want" are perfectly appropriate. If someone tells you to run out in the street or take drugs, shout with all your might: "I do not want to do that, and I will not do that, and I am going to tell my dad!" But most of the time, those phrases are not very helpful.

At first this will be tougher than you think. But once you put your mind to it, you will have no problem. You will be amazed how this helps you in your pursuit of happiness. Little effort, huge return, and you get ice cream! That is the model for smart investing. How cool is that?

Love,

Dad

SOLUTION THINKING

ACTIVITY TYPE

This is a creative journaling activity, designed to help you discover that there are solutions for every challenge. The solutions you come up with in this activity might be a strategy to make difficult tasks easier, or they might be the "next greatest invention."

Regardless, all solutions are your attempt to answer the same universal question. "How can I make this better?"

SUPPLIES FOR BOTH OF US

• 2 spiral notebooks, one for you and one for me

• 2 writing pens

INSTRUCTIONS FOR BOTH OF US

1) For one week, log in the spiral notebooks every frustrating experience, no matter how big or small. "I don't like the clothes I am wearing." Log it. "I don't like what is being cooked for dinner." Log it. Log everything that "tweaks." Each tweak needs to be logged on its own page at the top, along with the date. There will be a lot of white space on each page. Don't worry, more details will be added later.

2) At the end of the week, share the tweaks with one another.

3) Repeat steps 1 and 2 for one more week.

4) On the third week, pick five of the most troublesome tweaks.

5) Brainstorm together how to make those five tweaks better. Write down at least 3 solutions in the white space below the tweak. Skip a few lines between each solution. There is only one rule. Your solutions cannot include trying to control how someone else acts. *Love, you really need to think about this. Everything can be "fixed."*

6) Evaluate each solution for effort, cost, and the benefit. You can use a number scale or words. For example, effort = low, cost = low, benefit = high.

7) Rate your solutions from best to worst, with "1" being best. Write your ratings to the left of each solution. *Hint: a solution with high effort, high cost, and low benefit is probably not the best solution.*

 8) For the next 3 weeks, implement the top 2 solutions, unless of course the solution is an invention. In the case of an invention, spend some time writing down ideas on how to create that invention. During this 3-week period, share with the other any observations you have about your solutions.

WHY THIS MATTERS

On some days, you will experience something that just sucks.

I wish there was a word in the English language for what I am trying to describe, but there isn't. "Suck" is the best I can come up with.

It might be letting a fart slip out in the middle of a class, or it might be a daily task such as brushing your teeth. *Your little sister can't stand to take naps, but we all know she should!*

The will be no shortage of these sucky events. There is an abundance of things that will just stick you in the gut and frustrate you. Bullying your way through those frustrations rarely works. You have to be creative. Everyone should brush their teeth, but not everyone can succeed at brushing their teeth in the same manner. You have to find what works for you.

Every challenge is an opportunity for you to make improvements. If you do nothing, then you are rendering yourself powerless, and you will suffer.

When you were an infant, there was no problem that you could not solve. Reclaim that quality, and use it for the rest of your life. Doing so, will give you a life of power, abundance, freedom, and choice.

Love,

Dad

TAMING THE IMAGINATION

ACTIVITY TYPE

This is a mental exercise, designed to help take control of your imagination. Have you ever heard the phrase "Her imagination ran wild"?

Your imagination can act like a wild animal, on the hunt and going crazy. Sometimes it can feel as if your imagination is thinking on its own.

You have many emotions, but you have three primary states of mind. You are either in a good, neutral, or bad place.

When you are in a good place, you might be very excited about some upcoming event. You might be very excited about something that has just happened. Or, everything in your life is just rocking. It seems that everything is exceptional. You are "in the zone."

A neutral place is right in the middle between good and bad. You are unaware of anything exciting or challenging going on. You don't feel up, and you don't feel down. You are "coasting."

When you are in a bad place, you might be very angry or very sad. You might be very scared of something that is about to happen. Or you might be upset about something that just happened. Everything seems to go wrong. You are "in a funk."

Of course, there are infinite shades in between each of those three states. Think of those states like the three primary colors red, blue, and yellow. By mixing those three colors, millions of colors can be created. But, for this exercise, we will just talk about those three states of mind.

This exercise will help create awareness about your imagination while you are in the zone, coasting, or in a funk. Having this awareness will allow you to use your imagination in a healthy matter no matter how you are feeling at any moment.

SUPPLIES FOR BOTH OF US

• 2 calendars, one for you and one for me

• 2 spiral notebooks

• 2 writing pens

• About 100 small stickers that will represent the "good place"

• About 100 small stickers that will represent the "neutral place"

• About 100 small stickers that will represent the "bad place"

INSTRUCTIONS FOR BOTH OF US

1) Hang the calendar on the bedroom wall.

2) Every morning after awakening, place a sticker on the top half of the current day that best represents the state of mind at that moment. Every evening, before bed, place a sticker on the bottom of the current day that best represents the state of mind at that moment. Do this for seven days. *Don't self-judge for bad days.*

3) On the evening of the eighth day, continue placing stickers as before. Also, start writing very short journal entries in the spiral notebook. Journal entries should include the date, followed by three short sentences. The beginning of each sentence has been started for you below. All you need to do is complete each sentence.

- The most wonderful part of today was. . .
- Tonight, as I am falling asleep, I am going to imagine. . .
- When I awaken, I am going to lie in bed and imagine. . .

4) Repeat steps 2 and 3 until you run out of stickers.

RULES FOR BOTH OF US

1) No matter what kind of day is experienced, there is always some part of that day that was wonderful. The wonderful part of the day that is written about in the journal cannot include rejoicing in difficulty experienced by others.

2) Whatever is imagined when falling asleep or when awakening can only include what is desired. No "don't wants" allowed.

3) When in a funk, it is very difficult to use the imagination to blast an emotional state all the way to the good place. Therefore, during those times, try to experience imaginings that are smaller and easier to believe.

Baby steps, my love. Our only goal is to feel a little better, not a lot better.

WHY THIS MATTERS

When you are in a good place, imagination comes easy and it happens a lot, seemingly all by itself. It can be a great feeling. It is also hard for your imagination to rip you from that good place and put you in a bad place, but it is possible.

What is more likely, however, is that your imagination could gradually move you to that neutral place. Some people call this "coming back down to reality."

I don't like that phrase one bit.

When you are in a neutral place, imagination doesn't come as easy, and it happens a lot less. You can go for days without choosing to use your imagination. You just don't think about it. You wake up, do what you must do, and you go to bed.

But, it is easy for your imagination to get triggered by some outside event, and push you toward the good place or the bad place. *Keep that in mind when you are in a neutral place. It will help with some of choices you make.*

When you are in a bad place, your imagination is like it is when you are in a good place. It comes easy and it happens a lot, seemingly all by itself. The difference is that the imagination from a bad place oftentimes creates awful feelings.

It is hard for your imagination to lift you from that bad place and put you in a good place, but it is possible.

What is more likely, however, is that your imagination could gradually move you to that neutral place. People call this "getting out of a funk."

I like that phrase.

Pay close attention to what you think about, no matter how you are feeling. Make conscious choices about your thoughts. And if you find it difficult to choose good thoughts during difficult times, distract yourself with silly stuff like watching videos kittens, puppies or babies. *It really works.* In just a little short while, you will find it easier to choose your thoughts.

Love,

Dad

TALKING 'BOUT MIRACLES

ACTIVITY TYPE

This is a research activity, combined with a little presentation practice. Miracles are all around us, happening all the time. We are each going to research four miracles over the course of four weeks. At the end of each week, we will share what we learned about that week's miracle with each other.

SUPPLIES AND RESOURCES FOR BOTH OF US

- 2 spiral notebooks, one for you and one for me

- 2 writing pens

- access to information, such as the internet

INSTRUCTIONS FOR BOTH OF US

1) At the start of the first week, research and select a miracle that involved the weather.

2) For the remainder of the first week, research the miracle and jot down notes in the spiral notebook. If science has theorized how the miracle occurred, write down the theory.

3) At the end of the week, do a mini-presentation for one another.

4) Repeat this process a second week, selecting a miracle that involved an animal.

5) Repeat a third week, selecting a miracle that involved health, healing, or an escape from death.

6) Repeat a fourth week, selecting a miracle that involved a vision.

WHY THIS MATTERS

The older most people become, the more cynical they are. In a sense, they think of themselves as a pinball, bounced around in a life full of random coincidences. They believe life happens to them, instead of one that is created by their own thoughts. They are proving my point, that life follows thoughts, even stinky ones.

Do not fall into this trap. Life happens for you and because of you, so take control of your thoughts. One way to hold on to this belief to is acknowledge that miracles are everywhere.

Love,

Dad

A WATER CYCLE SCIENCE EXPERIMENT

ACTIVITY TYPE

This is a science experiment designed to demonstrate the miraculous water cycle. We are going to set up an environment that displays all four processes in the water cycle: collection, evaporation, condensation, and precipitation. This experiment will take about 10 minutes to set-up, and several hours just waiting for the sun and water to work their magic.

SUPPLIES

- Iodized salt
- Bottled drinking water
- Heavy ceramic cup or mug

- Large glass bowl, wide and tall enough to fit the cup completely inside
- Plastic cling wrap
- A stack of about 6 quarters taped together
- Sun

INSTRUCTIONS

1) Pour the drinking water into the cup or mug so that it's about 1 inch deep.

2) Mix about a spoonful of salt into the water. Stir it around and taste a tiny drop. If it is salty, great. If not, add a little more. Add enough so the water tastes salty. If you need to add a little more water because you took too many tastes, add enough to get the water level back to 1 inch deep.

3) Pour the salty water from the cup into the bowl.

4) Rinse the cup and dry it. Make sure that there is no salt residue in the cup.

5) Place the cup in the center of the bowl.

6) Cover the bowl tightly with the plastic cling wrap. Make sure that there are no open spots around the rim of the bowl.

7) Find a place that gets a lot of sunshine. This could be by a window, or even outside. If outside, make sure it is in a safe place and out of the way of walkers, joggers, or animals. Put the bowl down wherever you think it will get the most amount of sun.

8) Place the stack of quarters on top of the plastic wrap in the very middle, right above the cup. The quarters should cause the plastic wrap to sag in the center above the cup. When the water starts to vaporize, the plastic wrap is going to puff out, a little like a balloon. The quarters will ensure that the water drips off the plastic right above the cup.

cellophane stretched across bowl –
needs to be able to sag in the middle

coins on top of cellophane

cup

bowl

salt water in bottom of bowl

9) Go do something else for a couple of hours, but look in on the experiment occasionally.

10) You should notice water condensing on the underside of the plastic wrap. You might also notice drops of water falling into the cup, where your quarters were placed. Once the cup has enough water in it for you to take a small sip, take off the plastic wrap and remove the cup.

11) Drink the water. It's now pure and salt free!

WHY THIS MATTERS

Nothing on this planet is destroyed. The form of a particular thing might change, as well as the way it is used, but it is not destroyed. This is easy to understand when we think about physical stuff.

A shrimp eats some pond weed, a frog eats the shrimp, a fish eats the frog. Every one of those things that were eaten provided nutrients to the one that ate them. And after dinner, the shrimp, frogs, and fish that are still swimming around are going to pee and poop.

Guess what loves the pee and poop? The pond weeds and all of the other living plants in the water. All of the plants then make more plants, and the cycle continues.

Farmers spread cow poop on their crops to help them grow. Yep, the veggies and fruits that you eat were fed by pee, poop, and rotting stuff.

Water is used over and over, and over and over. The water today is the same water that was used by cavemen and dinosaurs, including the water in their pee!

But all that stuff is physical stuff that you can touch. What about the stuff that you can't touch? What about your spirit?

The part that makes you who you are and me who I am – our one-of-a-kind unique personality and spirit is no different than water, or anything else. It is an energy, a very powerful energy. And energy cannot be destroyed.

Think of yourself as eternal, because you are. Living life with this knowledge makes it a very different and more fulfilling experience than one that is lived without that knowledge.

Someday our bodies will be transformed into dirt, helping other creatures and plants come into existence. But you and I, we will be together forever in away that matters most... in spirit.

Love,

Dad

Acknowledgments

I am very grateful for my life and everyone in it. As I look at my life in retrospect, I now realize that I can really do nothing on my own. I am pretty sure this is true for many people.

Allow me to say thanks to all those who have been part of the different experiences throughout my time here on earth; the good, bad, and ugly. Thank you for shaping me in to the person I am today.

Lee Godwin, Chris LeBlanc, Neal McComas, Robert Lockhart, Buddy Bergeron, David Shipley, Pam Bergosh, Craig Herrod, Doug Stewart and Ed Ricks; I love every one of you, and cherish our friendship. You are more than friends to me. You are masterminds.

Many of the conversations we have shared over the years helped me sculpt and develop ideas into meaningful forms. Thank you for lending me your ears, minds, and thoughts.

Will Ackerman, Sara Wells, Cindy Hardy, and Heidi McComas; your comments were critical when this book was in its early form; fragmented, and lacking focus.

Thank you all for being a part of this experience, and the significant impact you had on this book.

My dear brother Mark Griffith; we have had an abundance of conversations about the topics in this book. Without exception, you always gave me your full attention, reaching deep in to your spirit.

Your insight, wisdom, and perspective is that of a soul who is 10,000 years old. You are a gift to this world. Thank you for exploring "the realm of thought" with me. I am blessed to have you as my brother. I love you brother.

Judy Griffith, wife and soul mate of my father, and my "bonus" mom. As I worked through this book, I was always eager to share my progress with you.

I could hardly wait to hear your thoughts on anything I shared. You are the most loving, forgiving, creative, and hopeful person I have ever encountered. Thank you, thank you, thank you for your feedback. I love you "Nana" Judy.

Ralph Zuranski, the impact you have had on my life and book is immeasurable. I liken our seemingly coincidental meeting of one another – we both know there is no such thing – to stumbling across a treasure chest with unbelievable riches.

I sought you out for a very narrow purpose. What I found instead was a talented editor, a master of writing style, a person of like mind that believes in the human potential to do good, and a friend.

Your "In Search of Heroes" program is a testament to the type of man you are, and the love you have for others. Thank you for making this book real. I could not have done it without you my friend. I love you dear friend.

Mark Foster, you are among the most gifted artists I have ever encountered. Your ability to "see" the design when given nothing more than a few sketchy ideas is incredible.

You gave yourself to this project for no other reason than the love that we share as friends. You give and you give and you give. You are a rarity among people.

Thank you for sharing your incredible gift with me, and helping this dream of mine come true. You made this book more than I thought it could be. You transformed it into a work of art. I love you brother.

Shade, Reese and Harmony, my amazing daughters! I have said it many times, you are my greatest teachers. It was your births that defined me as a father, your father, and you taught and are still teaching me, how to be a better father, your father.

No matter what I achieve in this life, being your father will always be the greatest achievement of my life. Thank you for choosing me to be your dad. I love you, I love you, and I love you. . . forever.

Yudy Maldonado, my new wife and my best friend, throughout this endeavor, you have given me your ears, eyes, heart and mind. You have been supportive, and made helping me finish this book a priority.

You have this incredible gift for seeing things objectively from the perspective of a parent. You are the most real person I have known. I am blessed to be your husband. You keep me grounded. Without you, this book would not have been completed. Thank you for your love and support. I love you.

Mom (Patricia Jordan), among my fondest memories are those of you reading Desiderata or the essays of Ralph Waldo Emerson to me when I was a young teen. You instilled in me the values of perseverance, hopefulness, kindness, gentleness, tenderness, compassion, self-reliance, and more.

Your life has been an incredible expression of those same values. You should be proud of your beneficial impact on me and your other children.

I am honored and blessed to have you as my mother. The sacrifices you made for me and my three brothers, instilled in me the same desire to lay my life down for others.

I love my children. You know this. You should take pride in my dedication to them. You helped shape me into the man and father I have become. Thank you mom! This book is a testament to the way you raised me. I love you Mom.

Dad (Dr. Paul Gene Griffith), words are inadequate to express the gratitude I feel for you. You are loving, brilliant, insightful, philosophical, whimsical, analytical, ethical, moral, multi-cultural, scientific, mathematical, architectural, experimental, musical, fun, inquisitive, methodical, tough as nails, and gentle. I could fill pages with words that describe you.

Even though you are no longer living here on this earth, I am still learning from you. As I was writing this book, I was flooded with our memories from my childhood.

There were so many things that you said that I did not fully understand until recently. It is as if you packed the inside of my mind with a bunch of seeds; seeds waiting for just the right time to germinate.

Your spirit is contained within the pages of this book. Thank you for the profound influence you had and are still having upon me. I cherish the daily conversations we have in the spirit. I love you Dad.

About Me

My name is John Griffith. I am a proud father, and primary parent of three daughters. For most of their lives, I have been a single parent.

I am an accomplished pianist and composer. I also possess advanced technology skills. *In case you did not know, that combination is very common.*

I grew up in the high plains of west Texas. I am well educated, but don't have any impressive letters at the end of my name such as Ph.D. But that's okay. The only distinction I really care about are the letters "DAD." For me personally, those mean everything.

I have three brothers. . . no sisters. During my elementary school years, I had more bloody noses, broken bones, stitches and broken teeth in any given year than there were months. I was just a "normal" boy. In fact, I was a "normal" boy all the way through my college days.

This beginning of this book contains more detail about these years of my life. When I shared those pages with a few trusted individuals, they made these gasping sounds as their heads shook from side to side. They were girls, so I interpreted their gyrations as confirmation that I was a "normal" boy.

After I graduated college, I decided to go on a quest to find myself. Instead of finding myself, I got lost. Really lost. Hopelessly lost. I was no longer a "normal" boy. If it wasn't for the birth of my first daughter in 1998, I am confident that my life would have ended before the new millennium.

Seriously. It is still difficult for me to reconcile the man I was before the she was born, with the man I became after she was born. It was a radical transformation.

If pairing dads with their first child was done via a selection process by some committee of "good" parents, I would have been an unlikely choice. But that's ok. I am in good company. The greatest stories we humans tell are the triumphs of the underdog against seemingly insurmountable odds.

Nobody believed David could defeat Goliath. The Continental Army should not have prevailed against the armies of the British Empire in the American Revolution. In the 1980 Winter Olympic Games, the USA hockey team defeated the heavily-favored Soviets and brought home the gold medal in the event that became known as "The Miracle on Ice." Who saw that coming?

Just like you, and everyone else on this planet, I was born a naturally happy baby. And like everyone else on this planet (and maybe you too), I lost that happiness as I grew older.

If you don't believe that we lose our happiness as we grow older, go watch elementary school children playing at a park. You will probably find yourself smiling. Next, go to an airport or a mall, and watch the adults in their "playground." Those are some sad, guarded, worrisome, defensive, selfish folks.

What kind of life is that? Surely that is not how life is supposed to be.

Before my first daughter was born, I was one of those sad, guarded, worrisome, defensive, selfish folks. But then some amazing things happened.

I became a parent of a baby girl. Words cannot begin to describe that miraculous, life-altering moment. And then, a few weeks after she was born, she knocked me out emotionally. It is an incredible story which you can read about in the beginning of this book.

Come on now, you can't really expect me to spoil your joy of discovery before you read my entire book?

Those experiences marked the beginning of my reawakening, a new journey that continued for many years. In fact, it is still evolving as I am now raising three daughters. Throughout my years of "DAD" training, and thanks to my daughters, I gradually identified the stinking, thinking patterns that caused me to drift. Today, I am joyful, grateful, and my happiness is restored.

I wrote this book as a gift to my three daughters, and other family members. But now that it is finished, keeping this wisdom within my family circle is no longer an option. I have to share my discoveries with you.

We live in a society where the media (unintentionally) works against our happiness. We are constantly bombarded by a stream of "Bad News." We are encouraged to find power in suffering and entitlement. Addictive behavior is sensationalized and glamorized. Many in the media promote lying, deception, and revenge. *Heck, we are even taught how to get away with murder.*

Have you ever wondered, "Where are the messages regarding the amazing power of choice, personal responsibility, and accountability?" Why isn't every person told they are responsible for their own happiness?"

And that brings me to the crux of the matter.

We can't do much about the focus of the media. Smut sells. But that is okay. It is not the media's duty to provide our children with the tools necessary for a happy life.

Dads and moms, that is our job. We are the ones to show our children how to remain happy while living in a society replete with smutty messaging. But we don't have a chance at raising a happy child, if we ourselves are not happy.

We parents are (potentially) our children's most powerful influencers. Our support, guidance and love can dramatically impact their lives, despite the messaging that works against their happiness. What an awesome opportunity we have!

In addition to my three daughters Shade, Reese and Harmony, I have one adult son (Aaron), whom I adopted just before going on the quest described above.

I missed his growing up years because I guess I was trying to grow up too. Now I am learning how to connect with an adult son that I forsake during most of his childhood. He is beautiful, open-hearted, kind, sensitive, witty, humorous, and loving. He has been amazing in his response and his willingness to open his heart to me. Nothing is ever lost in this life; there are only gains to be had. But Aaron has chosen to expand those gains. He is remarkable.

I recently remarried an incredible woman and now have her and two stepsons to add to the family. I will never write a book on marriage, but I might write one about remarriage. I will probably give it the title *If at First You Don't Succeed, Try, Try, Try and Try Again; The Marriage I Finally Got Right*.

Thank you for making our world a better place by reading and sharing this book with your children, family and friends!

Index